true stories from

an unreliable

eyewitness

—————————
—————————

true stories from an unreliable eyewitness

A Feminist Coming of Age

CHRISTINE LAHTI

HARPER WAVE

An Imprint of HarperCollins*Publishers*

The names and identifying characteristics of some of the individuals featured throughout this book have been changed to protect their privacy.

HarperCollins books may be purchased for educational, business, or sales promotional use. For information, please email the Special Markets Department at SPsales@harpercollins.com.

FIRST EDITION

Library of Congress Cataloging-in-Publication Data has been applied for.

ISBN 978-0-06-266367-2
ISBN 978-0-06-285617-3 (B&N Signed Edition)
ISBN 978-0-06-285814-6 (B&N Signed Mother's Day Edition)

18 19 20 21 22   LSC   10 9 8 7 6 5 4 3 2 1

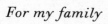

For my family

"Memory is a complicated thing, relative to the truth but not its twin."

—*Barbara Kingsolver*

"Any woman who chooses to behave like a full human being should be warned that the armies of the status quo will treat her as something of a dirty joke. . . . She will *need* her sisterhood."

—*Gloria Steinem*

"A dysfunctional family is any family with more than one person in it."

—*Mary Karr*

CONTENTS

Introduction: Why Write Now? (Click)   XI

1. Free John Funky   1

2. The Smile of Her   7

3. Make-Believer   25

4. Hidden   35

5. Walking   39

6. Shit Happens   51

7. The Wet Towel   59

8. The Street Where "They" Lived   67

9. Mississippi Baby   77

10. Losing Virginity   87

11. Kidnapped   97

12. What I Wish I'd Known About Love Scenes 107

13. Brave 117

14. Dear Pregnant Women of a Certain Age . . . 123

15. Running on Empty 131

16. Panic 141

17. Brother 147

18. Monster 159

19. Mamma Mia 167

20. Waiting 189

Acknowledgments 199

Why Write Now? (Click)

THIS BOOK IS a collection of my true stories. They are my emotional memories, the goo that surrounds the facts, the parasitic muck that attaches to them. These are the stories that altered me in some way, even just temporarily. They chronicle events when something inside me stirred or quaked. There was a shift in my focus. A tremor up my spine. A hot flash of injustice, of shame. A humble reckoning with my own imperfections. An acceptance. A forgiveness.

Some of these stories have made me fight harder. Others are lessons I keep having to relearn; taking three steps backward and wobbling before being able to stand up straight again. Sometimes these stories are simply a quiet reminder of hope when everything in me wanted to give up. These are the kind of memories that have been permanently etched into my psyche.

My siblings, upon reading some of them, cried foul. "What? I don't remember that at all!" or "That's not how they happened!" That's because, as sifted through my personal filter, these events didn't happen to them. In fact, my first story, "Free John Funky," concerns the fallibility of memory; how emotion can sometimes render us unreliable eyewitnesses to our own true stories.

Even so, I've found value in telling the stories that those memories have, over the years, solidified into. Most of mine occupy a place where comedy and tragedy overlap. In that regard, my life has often felt like a Chekhov play, albeit one set in an affluent Detroit suburb and then migrating to New York and Los Angeles.

Many of these stories are told through the lens of my ever-evolving feminism, the lens through which I see just about everything. I call them my click moments. Back in the 1970s, I was told that I would have only one click; the moment when my feminism dropped bone-deep, from my head into my body. A eureka moment from which there could be no turning back. The veil would be permanently lifted. I'd see the world in a completely different way, and it would turn me into a lifelong activist.

Part of that turned out to be true. My first big awakening is described in the story "Walking," but I've had hundreds of clicks. I've been a clumsy feminist, finding solid footing only to be knocked down again. And I keep finding new veils to be lifted.

The order of these stories loosely follows that stumbling journey to find agency—from innocence toward experience, from powerlessness toward empowerment. I see this collection as the highs and lows of a feminist who is very much still a work in progress, with all the humiliating, hilarious, heartbreaking potholes along the way.

IN COLLEGE CHESTER MARTIN, an older professional actor who I deeply respected, looked at me through watery, bloodshot eyes and told me I had no light to shed upon the human existence and that I would never make it as an actress. Never mind that he was sloshed and that I had just rejected his inappropriate, aggressive sexual advances. Nevertheless I believed him, and it crushed me. Not for long, though, because I decided soon after that no matter what he thought, I *had* to act. I saw the film *Long Day's Journey into Night*, directed by Sidney Lumet, at the State Theatre in Ann Arbor, Michigan, in the autumn of 1970. Unable to stop sobbing, I rode my bike around campus for an hour afterward. I knew by the end of that ride that I needed to be part of films, plays, and stories that would have that kind of power to move people.

I grew up in a family of six children, four girls and two boys, in Birmingham, Michigan. I was the third oldest. Dad was a busy general surgeon. Mom was a full-time housewife who later became a professional artist. I was born a drama queen, someone with extreme emotions, which didn't always sit so well in a family that was emotion-phobic and prone to stoicism.

Mom graced us with unconditional love, while Dad's love seemed conditional on how successful we were. Hence, I became obsessed with accomplishment. I found theater in the sixth grade: I played the Virgin Mary in the Christmas pageant and a tree in the school play. I loved being able to step inside the skin (or bark) of different characters. But I especially appreciated the applause. It felt like a hundred of my dads clapping just for me.

I attended the University of Michigan, where I originally majored in languages thanks to a fantasy of working as a translator at the UN. But I quickly switched to theater by my sophomore year. As it was the late 1960s, I also de facto majored in being an activist and hippie. The second wave of feminism was just beginning to emerge in my world, and I would leave Ann Arbor in 1972 a radically different person from the conservative girl who'd entered college as a freshman in 1968.

Before that, I'd never really noticed gender inequality. It was just "the way things were." Then I started seeing sexism and misogyny lurking, like vermin, in every corner. For the first time, I felt the chronic grip of patriarchy. It was like when I got glasses in sixth grade. I had no idea that my world had always been out of focus. Then instantly, everything became shockingly clear.

I moved to New York City in 1973 to study acting. To pay my rent, I started waitressing at places like the Improv (where I threw a drink at Jimmie Walker onstage because he made a comment about my breast size) and the Quiet Little Table in the Corner, where I discovered that businessmen were getting blow-job lunches from their secretaries behind the beaded curtains of their booths. I also did mime in Central Park for tips. Yup, I was one of *those* incredibly irritating people.

Then, while making my dutiful rounds, trying to find

an agent, I met with an alcoholic one who told me my
dreams were much too big for my britches. "Not special
enough and too tall," I could never be a "serious" actress.
Apparently most male stars were short and would never
agree to work opposite the likes of monster-me. *His* career
advice was that I should move out to LA to do sitcoms.
Back then advising an actress to go to LA to do sitcoms was
like advising her to become a lap dancer.

I became determined to prove him and all my other
naysayers wrong: I would do whatever it took to make
them eat their words. I went on to study with the finest
teachers I could find: Uta Hagen, Bill Esper, and Stella
Adler. I started getting parts in plays off-off-Broadway,
which became my training ground. Cockroaches and mice
frequently shared the stage with me. After I got my first
professional acting job and Equity card, I remember silently thanking all those discouraging men. I'm still thanking them.

I got married in 1988, and my husband and I had our
first child four years later. After living in the New York
City theater world for twenty years, we moved to the film
and TV world of Los Angeles. Just for two years. Which
somehow turned into twenty. We raised our three children
there, and the second they went away to college, we became bicoastal.

Now, having worked as an actress and director for nearly
forty years, I'm in my mid-sixties, and the more exciting
acting offers have gotten fewer and farther between. What
the fuck's that about? I naively asked myself just ten years
ago. Why are there so few great parts for women in their

fifties and sixties? Aren't our stories more interesting than ever? There's a shelf life for actresses? These thoughts hadn't really occurred to me in my younger years, while I watched successful male actors continue working into their late seventies, sometimes as the leading man. I know. My capacity for denial has surprised even me sometimes.

So maybe I'm not "fuckable" anymore (a word that always makes me want to say "Then don't fuck with me!"), but I'm in my creative prime. I'm finally fully charged, at the top of my game, and *now* I'm supposed to shut up? Nope, not gonna happen.

In recent years, I've been feeling, more than ever, the powerlessness inherent in acting. Actors are dependent on other people to be creative. After all, it's not much fun acting by ourselves. How many times can we perform monologues? Who is going to applaud? Do we make a laugh track and just run it on a loop? Where the hell do we perform? In front of our dogs? In a closet so the neighbors don't call the police? I'd rather give lap dances.

When I teach acting master classes, I always tell my students, especially the young women, that they must become a quadruple threat: they should not only act but also write, direct, and produce. They must create their own projects and generate their own work. I find that many in this younger generation already intuitively understand this. In fact, quite a lot of them seem as if they were raised with an agency they didn't have to struggle for years to find. (I like to think having feminist mothers had something to do with that.)

But in the past, whenever encouraged to start my own

production company, I always used to say, "Oh no, I'm not entrepreneurial like that!" Finally, in my sixties, I started developing projects and producing. I think it's safe to say I'm a late bloomer.

Then, inspired by the urging of my kick-ass twenty-two-year-old daughter, feminist husband, and several close friends, I started to write. Holy motherfucking click. Why did I wait so long?

These stories cover three main periods: my childhood, my early journey as an actress and activist, and adulthood. "The Smile of Her" charts the evolution of my mother's smile and how I became a feminist in spite of and because of it. My mother has given me a wellspring of treasured clicks. In many ways I feel I'm living her unlived life.

Clicks can come in many forms. Like in the form of a hooker on Eighth Avenue who inadvertently changes your day or a sleazy casting director who says you can't "make it" unless you become a prostitute. "Walking" and "Waiting" follow me along my long path to find agency, particularly in the sexist world of show business. "Mamma Mia" is about the power of empowering someone else, even when I deeply disagree with her choice. "Running on Empty" attempts to understand my father—how he, like most men of his generation, was limited by a narrow definition of masculinity. In "Brave," "Panic," and "Shit Happens," an earthquake, a panic attack on the other side of the world, and a nearly missed Golden Globe serve to pull the rug out from under my chronic need to be perfect, a need that started when growing up as a girl felt like a liability and being flawless seemed the surest way to win respect. You could call me a respect junkie—but respect from others never gave me the kind of agency I was searching for.

Now, as an adult, I've discovered that embracing my imperfections has brought me closer to what I'd really been seeking all along: self-respect. For me, true agency began once I was able to accept all the ways I actually suck. These stories chart that growth from "perfect" to imperfect; as a feminist, a mother, a wife, a daughter, an actress, and a drama queen.

I may not have much "light to shed on the human existence," but I sure have come to adore the light beckoning me from my computer screen. It invites me to create with autonomy. It's been scary at times, but also cathartic—and I love that I can do it with no makeup, and not even a trace of Botox. Although as I type this, staring at my veiny hands, I can't help but think what a little filler could do to plump them up. Just the tiniest bit.

true stories from

an unreliable

eyewitness

_____

_____

Free John Funky

JUST CAN'T BE 100 percent sure anymore that it didn't come out of *my* butt.

I was in first grade, sitting at our writing table, minding my own business, happily practicing my cursive with my freshly sharpened No. 2 pencil. On my left sat my classmate, the unfortunately named John Funky. Short and soft-looking, this fellow had cauliflower ears and a freakishly premature receding hairline. Just as I was making the final swirl in my capital L in Lahti, I smelled something horrible. I looked under our table, and on the floor, right next to John Funky's feet, sat a couple of fresh human turds. My hand shot up into the air like a missile. I waved it frantically. Our teacher rushed over, and I informed her of this disgusting, law-breaking shenanigan.

"Miss Beasley, somebody had an accident on the floor!" I said with an urgency that a lit stick of dynamite under the table might have warranted. Miss Beasley, a skinny tree of a woman with a permanent prunelike wince on her face, hissed through clenched yellow teeth, "Where? Who did it?"

My trembling finger pointed at the poo. Then at John. She looked down. She gasped. "MISTER FUNKY! Clean up those stools NOW!" John got up, staring at the floor. His cheeks reddened. He fetched the broom and dustpan and swept up the mess. He was then banished to the principal's office or wherever kids went to be punished for shitting on the floor of their classrooms.

Okay. I've told that "John Funky" story hundreds of times since I was a kid.

But now, at sixty-five years old, I've discovered that some memories have become a little loose at the seams. For example, not so long ago, I was shocked to find out that my brother and sister barely remembered a terrifying family trip when our dad kicked our mom out of the car in downtown Chicago. How could something so seared into my brain be merely a blip on the childhood radar for them? Did my siblings omit the parts that were too painful for them? Did I exaggerate them because of my own fears? Memory is, by nature, subjective and therefore flawed. So am I not to be trusted to tell my own impactful stories? Even though I was there? In person and close up?

LET US FIRST examine the facts. This much I know to be true: Miss Beasley's class wasn't some ordinary teacher's first-grade class. In her room, if and when she detected something in the air that just "wasn't right," Miss Beasley would conduct her signature "coatroom checks."

"One, two, three, all eyes on me! All right children, I need all the boys to line up in the coatroom, please," she announced, her face cracking with the tiniest hint of pleasure.

With hushed groans, the boys filed in. Knowing the drill, they marched to their assigned coat hook, faced the back wall, bent over, and dropped their trousers, keeping on their tighty-whities. Then Miss Beasley would stroll by each one of them and with slow, deep inhales, as if she were in a cooking class inspecting freshly made muffins, she . . . sniffed. If she found the guilty party, she hurried him off to the principal's office. If she didn't, she barked the most dreaded words that could come out of a teacher's mouth:

"All right, boys may return to their seats. I need all the girls to line up, please."

Then it was our turn to enter that lion's den. We went to our coat hooks and faced the wall, but since we weren't allowed to wear pants, we had to lift our skirts or dresses and bend over. Miss Beasley, once again walking in slow motion, checked and smelled each of our backsides.

It's a good thing for Miss Beasley that this happened in 1957. If she behaved like this today, she'd be stuck having to sniff the underwear of her fellow inmates in the Michigan State Prison.

So given our perverted teacher, it's possible I felt a little anxious when I spotted those turds on the floor, but I also know for a fact that they were sitting right next to John's foot. His name was John Funky, people—of course he did it. Obviously! Miss Beasley believed me, and I have stood by this truth since I was six years old!

But now, sixty years later, maybe it is time to do some reexamination. Especially after a friend recently pointed out some gaping holes in my narrative.

First and most critically, he reminded me that John Funky must have been wearing trousers—long pants— given the strict dress codes of 1957. "So, Christine," my skeptical friend asked, "how did he get them off? How did the crap *get* to the floor, so very much intact? Even with the baggiest pants known to man, it would have been extremely difficult for him to just shake those bad boys all the way down his legs. However, because you were wearing a skirt or a dress, it would have been a lot easier for you just to . . . let them slip out, right?"

Now it had never in a million years occurred to me that *I* could have actually been responsible for this, but my friend's scenario started to make a little sense. He continued, "Christine, you had to go to the bathroom, but you were so deeply immersed in your beloved cursive practice that you didn't want to miss one second of it. So you simply let a couple drop and kicked them over toward John. Plus, given your teacher's depraved sniffing ritual, you felt desperate to blame someone else, and the closest target was poor Mr. Funky."

If *I* were investigating the veracity of my story, I would have to admit that around that same time in my life, I might have been a little prone to lying. I might also have been a bit of a tattletale and drama queen. I could cite as evidence against myself the time I was angry at my older sister Carol for some reason I can no longer remember. She was ten, I was eight. Standing at our orange laminate kitchen counter, she prepared her midday snack. As she meticulously poured her honey onto her open-faced peanut butter sandwich, I stuck my thumb into it and swirled it around, wrecking her obsessively perfect design.

"MAHHHHHH," taunted the devil that lived inside me. "I'm warning you, Chris. Don't you touch this sandwich again," she yelled as I headed for the hills. She resumed dripping her pathetic honey pattern. As she saw me coming back, she grabbed the knife she was using. Twisting her blade in the air as if she were gutting a mackerel, she made it crystal clear what she would do to me if I didn't obey.

But again I stuck my thumb in her sandwich and mushed it around. This time, as I bolted away, she flung the knife at me, hitting me in the shoulder. That stopped me in my tracks. *My sister just threw a knife at me.* I stomped into the powder room and lifted my T-shirt to examine the damage in the mirror. Disappointed, I noticed only a barely discernible pink mark that looked more like a flea bite than a stab wound. So I proceeded to scratch my back with my stubby fingernails over and over again, just to make sure my parents understood the full horror of the assault. Then, just as I was manufacturing some very real tears, I heard them come home and flung open the bathroom door.

"Mom, Dad, Carol threw a knife at me! Ow, look, I'm bleeding!" I tenderly touched my scratches for dramatic effect. As further proof, I showed them the dagger, which I'd confiscated from the kitchen floor. But little did I know at the time that this deadly weapon happened to be . . . a butter knife. My parents took one look at my angry red gouges, one look at the pitiful knife, and grounded *me* for two weeks.

Could I have so brazenly lied to Miss Beasley, as I did to my parents? Even at six years old, I knew I was supposed to be a good little girl and that pooping on the floor in class was not in my job description—especially in this particular classroom.

So at the behest of my friend, to potentially free Mr. Funky from any more shame and humiliation, I hereby allow the tiniest possibility that it could have been . . . me. If I falsely blamed him, I apologize, once and for all. John, if you're reading this, please forgive me. And who the hell knows, maybe it was a third kid who did it and just lobbed the crap over to us. What if it wasn't shit at all, but actually just some discarded brown Play-Doh?

Okay, clearly memories can be fallible and fluid, but does that mean I have to disavow all the stories that, over the years, I have reliably told myself and others? So what if some fiction gets mixed in with our "facts"? Maybe we need to protect ourselves from remembering experiences that threaten our sense of self.

But if more of my memories start shifting around like fault lines, will they cause tremors in my identity? Isn't our collection of memories the bedrock of who we are? Aren't our stories what give us hope and help us make sense of the world?

Fuck it. John Funky shat on the floor in first grade. It's my story, and I'm sticking to it.

2

The Smile of Her

DURING RECESS, AS I climbed up the big kid's slide, Corky Gordon yelled from below, "I see London. I see France. I see Chrissy's underpants." Instantly a dozen other kids on the playground swarmed around to gaze up my skirt.

After school, my wet eyes fixed on the sidewalk, I rushed home to my room and waited.

"Oh, yoo-hoooo! Yoodee-hoodee! I'm hooome!"

And as if by magic, all was right with the world. The six of us kids stopped whatever we were doing and came running. Even our dog started leaping into the air to catch a glimpse of my mother's ruby-red smile as she entered our house. Framed by two deep dimples and a glamorous black beauty mark, her smile seemed to light her from the inside out.

This was 1950s Birmingham, Michigan, an affluent, bucolic suburb of Detroit where everyone had swimming pools filled with water that our parents told us would turn purple if we peed in them. Mom was a housewife, and everybody adored her. If there had been a contest for most perky, she would have won it hands down. She gave her smile as a gift to everyone, whether they wanted it or not. Walking by her side, I watched with pride as people fell helpless under its spell.

Every morning we'd hear her in the kitchen, her voice like a chickadee: "Rise and shi-ine! Breakfast is ready!" Then she'd sing to my dad, "Here's your Sanka, darling. How are you on this ga-lor-i-ous day?"

Dad's head would be buried in the *Detroit Free Press* sports section, but he'd respond "Never felt better in my life" as he sucked the life out of his Meerschaum pipe. It's what he always answered, every time, no matter what.

"OH, FOR CHRIST'S sake, pipe down, will you, Betty? You're not making any sense!"

"See, you don't respect me. You won't even listen to me!"

I was in bed, under the covers, with all my stuffed animals and dolls. Just outside my door, in the hallway, a tornado was raging.

"Hey, I said pipe down, Betty!"

"Ahhh, I can't stand this! I'm sick of you always trying to shut me up!"

I dove down under my giant teddy bear and didn't hear any more. I pulled my Chatty Cathy doll's string to drown them out. "Please brush my hair, take me with you, I love you, please brush my hair, take me with you, I love you!"

Cathy pleaded. I'd never heard my parents fight before. I'd never, ever, heard my mom sound like this.

The next morning, wary of leftover debris from last night's storm, I went downstairs. "Hey, Dad. How're you doing?"

"Never felt better in my life!"

Mom chirped through her biggest, most excited smile, "Hi, honey! Want to get dolled up and go to the grocery store with me today?"

So there we were, two sparkly girls out shopping. I saw a floral dress with a white petticoat in the window of a clothing store. I stopped, dazzled by the wonder of it.

"Oh, Mommy! Look at all those red roses! Do you think we could—"

"Not today, honey."

"Please, Mommy, pleeease!"

"I'm sorry, Chrissy, but I just can't swing it."

"Oh please, look, it's on sale and I could wear it for my birthday party!"

"No, you don't understand, honey. Your dad . . . um . . . your dad took my credit cards away this morning."

"What? Why?"

"I misbehaved."

"You what?"

"I *misbehaved*, you know, honey, like when children get grounded sometimes? Like that."

"Oh, well, okay."

She took my hand. "But it doesn't mean we can't go get some yummy Neapolitan ice cream!"

I looked up at her million-dollar smile, and once again all was well.

WHEN MOM DIDN'T smile, it scared me. Her smile had become my barometer of well-being. There was the time she caught me teasing my older brother, mimicking his severe stutter. Her smile vanished. The room emptied of life, like a river gone dry. "You just wait until your father gets home," she said in her deepest voice. Translated, that meant *You just wait until your dad straps you with that leather belt of his!*

Then there were those times when, after a jam-packed day of being Super Mom, she'd fall asleep on the family room couch after sipping her Manhattan, collapsing around eight o'clock.

"Dad, Mom's snoring again," I'd whisper.

"Yeah, I can't hear the TV!" my brother would complain.

Dad would turn up the volume on *Father Knows Best*. "Ah, leave her alone, she's exhausted."

One of us would quietly ask, "Are you asleep, Mom?"

"Nope, just resting my eyes!" she'd respond, popping up, snapping to attention, her smile back intact, as if she'd been caught sleeping on the job.

Mom had much to be happy about, though. She was so proud of her brilliant, handsome surgeon husband, her six adorable children, and her traditional six-bedroom red-brick house with its grand front yard and circular driveway. Her favorite room was our all-white living room: white carpet, white furniture, white curtains. When she had parties, I'd overhear her friend, Penny, say "Oh my goodness, Betty, how do you do it? With all those rambunctious children and a dog in this house! Why on earth would you pick white?" Mom would just grin, never divulging her secret—the plastic she'd put on all the furniture during the day.

In addition, we kids and the dog were never allowed to enter the "living" room—which was clearly not meant for living—without permission, except for the rare times when relatives came over and we were invited in.

"Chrissy! Get over here, you little cutie-pie! Come give your auntie a big kiss!" bellowed my mom's sister, Barbara, her chin glistening in the sun-drenched room.

"Hi." I hovered in the doorway, my tiny grass-stained toes butting up against the forbidden carpet. It stretched out before me, perilous, like a swamp of hungry white crocodiles.

"Sweetie, don't be shy! It's fine!" said Mom.

"Ahh . . . uh, uh."

"Chrissy, it's okay. Come in!" Mom's smile grabbed me and pulled me in.

I took a deep breath and, as fast as I could, pranced over to them, barely letting my sticky feet brush the surface of the carpet. Mom scooped me up onto her lap, "It's okay, honey, I got you." Then she enveloped me into the body of her smile.

WHEN I WAS nine years old, Mom gave each of us four girls a laminated checklist headed "Good Grooming Habits for Young Ladies." They included brushing your hair fifty strokes every night, moisturizing elbows and knees daily, and tips on how to keep your smile bright and pretty. I followed them all dutifully. I'd brush my teeth as long as it took me to hum "Happy Birthday." Then I'd rehearse smiling in the mirror, jabbing my fingers into my cheeks, trying to make my dimples as deep as hers. I even created a beauty mark with one of her eyeliner pencils, though it looked more like a tick sucking on my face. Mom was the epitome of a lady, and I wanted to be just like her.

Until one day I walked in on her getting dressed.

I instantly looked away. "Whoa, Mom! What in the world are you doing?"

She was naked, squeezing into a full-size girdle from her ankles to her waist. Next, she hooked on a corset into which she was trying to stuff her six-children-plus-two-stillborns floppy stomach.

"Why are you wearing that?"

"Oh, it's fine, honey. See, I'm wearing slacks today."

"But why are you putting all that tight stuff under them?"

"Oh, this is a piece of cake! I'm used to this!"

Taking in little gasps of air, she pulled her stretch pants and sweater over the underarmor. If you want to be pretty like her, I thought, you just have to do this stuff. I knew that cooking and cleaning were her household duties, and that caring for us was crucial. But her beauty seemed to be an additional critical responsibility. Repeatedly, we heard "Eeek, close the windows, the hair, the hair!" or "I'll be right out! I just need to put my face on!" or "See, honey, how these jowls go away when I smile?" So there went

Mom, walking through her day, coiffed and jowl-free, in a head-to-toe girdle, unable to breathe.

IT WASN'T UNTIL I was about ten years old that I began to see Mom's perfected smile as something a bit more complicated.

"Betty, put out the cigarette, please." Dad had both hands on the faux-wood steering wheel of our Buick station wagon.

"What do you mean, Ted? I just lit it," she responded, taking in a deep breath of smoke.

"You shouldn't be smoking with all the kids in the car. You shouldn't be smoking at all." It was dusk. We were all packed in, having just visited the Chicago Science Museum, and it was snowing hard. What's the big deal? I thought. Mom always smokes in the car with us. How bad can it be?

"Just come down one time to my operating room, Betty, and see the black-tarred lungs of my patients." (This was a standing invitation for all of us; a "guaranteed smoking deterrent.")

But Mom kept puffing away. I had never seen her not obey my father.

"Betty, did you hear what I said?" The wipers scraped across our icy windshield. "Put the cigarette out now, Betty," he warned under his breath.

She kept smoking, the tension in the car as thick as the fumes.

"Either you put it out or you're getting out."

She just kept smoking. So Dad pulled the car over and

slammed on the brakes. Betty didn't move. With eyes locked straight ahead, she exhaled slowly, pushing out little ghosts of smoke that floated in the air around Dad's head.

"Get out now!" He leaned over and threw open the door, his slicked-back hair flying wildly around his reddened face. A shock of snow blew in.

"No, Mom! Don't leave! Close the door!"

But she got out. Holding down her hair with one hand, the other hand glued to her cigarette, she whacked the door shut with her hip. Dad zoomed off. From the far back seat of our station wagon, all I could see was her body getting smaller and smaller, until she disappeared altogether.

"Dad! No! Go back for her!"

But Dad kept driving. The longer he drove, the more certain I was that she'd be lost forever. Where will she go? I thought to myself. How will she find food? How will she fight off all the scavenging packs of rabid dogs that must roam this frozen city?

A few minutes later—though it felt like an eternity—he turned another corner. We saw Mom walking alone on a snow-covered sidewalk. He pulled up beside her, shifted over to the passenger seat, and opened the door. She threw down the last of her butt. It hissed as it hit the snow. She got in. Dad didn't say a word. Mom wouldn't look at him. She then planted a smile across her makeup-smeared face and looked back at our faces, which were overflowing with relief.

"Aw, your dad wouldn't have left me, kids," she said. "He was just mad at me and wanted to teach me a lesson.

I knew he'd come right back." But this time I chewed my cuticle, tasting a sting of blood. This misbehavior might not just get her credit cards taken away. She might be grounded forever.

ONE NIGHT, WHEN I was around fourteen, Mom sat with me on her bed after dinner. "You know, honey," she said, "I was the editor of my high school paper."

"What? Really, Mom?"

"Yes, and I won several literary awards and art contests," she said, focused on chipping off remnants of her nail polish.

"Mom, you never told me that. That's so great! Why don't you do any of that now?"

"Oh, no, honey, don't be silly. I love just being your mom! Maybe in another lifetime," she said with a little chuckle. Her smile looked a little strained now, its dimples less defined. She brushed bits of red polish off the floral peach bedspread into her matching wastepaper basket.

I WAS EIGHTEEN now, a senior in high school. My first boyfriend, the love of my life, Billy, was leaving my room, tucking in his shirt. He passed by Mom, who was standing just outside my door.

My father walked into my room. "Why buy the cow, Chris, when you can get the milk for free?" he whispered.

"What, Dad? I'm sorry . . . um . . . huh?"

"Trust me, all men want is one thing—to get into your pants. That's all they care about. So why buy the cow, if you can get the milk for free?" He spelled it out again, urgently, as if he were pointing out the exit doors in a theater engulfed in flames. The air in my tiny bedroom thickened. I couldn't wait for my father to leave. I stepped out into the hallway to see if Mom was still there. Startled, she slapped on one of her Betty Lahti smiles.

"Oh, uh . . . dinner's in ten minutes, sweetie." She turned and marched down our long hallway, leaving only whispers of her Chanel No. 5 lingering behind.

WHEN I SET off for the University of Michigan, with my properly moisturized elbows and knees, I promptly joined a sorority famous for its members' great success at finding husbands. It was what I knew. Mom and I took a picture together the day she came for our first Delta Gamma mother-daughter brunch. With our identical frozen smiles and color-coordinated silk scarves, we sat, legs crossed at the ankle, hands in our laps, as if patiently waiting for something exciting to happen.

Sunday evening, at the end of my first week there, a loud bell was rung. All the DGs were told to come down to the living room for the "candle ceremony." I expected it to be some kind of religious ritual.

"Oh, no!" my new blond "sister" Nancy explained. "See, we all stand in a circle, almost every week, and depending on how many times the candle goes around before it's blown out, someone is either going steady, getting lavaliered, or—drumroll, please—getting engaged!"

The candle completed the circle three times. When it was finally blown out, there was a kind of surreal sorority group orgasm. These smart young women with their promising futures crazily leaped upon the bride-to-be, hooting and hollering, as if she'd discovered the cure for cancer. The room, with its varying shades of designer beige, became cramped, almost claustrophobic. As I backed away from the circle of stretched lipstick smiles, I felt myself backing away from my mother for the first time.

A month later, I quit that sorority. I spent the rest of my college life protesting the Vietnam War, marching for civil rights, and going to women's consciousness-raising meetings. The status symbol in my new circle became a lump on the head from a cop's billy club, a far cry from the coveted poodle skirts of my youth. To me, Mom now looked like a Stepford wife. To her, I probably looked like someone who might at any moment burn their house down.

"JESUS CHRIST, MOM, what's wrong with you?"

"Why, what?" She touched her hair, capturing any strays that had escaped.

"Why are you smiling so much? It looks totally fake."

We were entering the grocery store during one of my obligatory visits home. She proceeded to chirp, "Hello, how are you?" to the cashier, the customers, the grocery bagger, and the produce man. "Hello! How's your wife? Love your dress! Oh my goodness, don't your tomatoes look absolutely sca-rumptious today!"

"Why are you being like this?" I said. "You don't know any of these people! Why are you being so cheery? Dad never even says hi to anyone."

"Well, gosh, honey, I don't know. I think I just like to

be friendly," she explained, her smile now as compliant as the supermarket doors that swung open whenever anyone came near.

"Mom, who are you going to vote for?" I suddenly challenged her.

"Oh, well, I don't know, honey. I guess whoever your dad votes for. Why?"

I walked away from her so she couldn't rub off on me, infectious like poison ivy.

AFTER COLLEGE, I moved to New York City, where I found myself saying, "Any woman who smiles a lot isn't paying fucking attention!" Determined not to be objectified, I refused to wear skirts or dresses. Makeup was absolutely out—except for auditions.

On a visit home, I feared the gap between Mom and me had become too wide to bridge. Nevertheless, I helped her in the kitchen, stirring a big pot of chili one evening. I knew it was time to let the bitch out of the bag. I watched her whole body deflate when I "came out" to her as . . . a feminist.

"Oh, honey. Does this mean you're a lesbian?"

"What? No, Mom!"

"Well, you don't seem to take pride in your appearance as you used to," she said mournfully. "And I can't help but notice you're not shaving your legs."

"Mom, that has nothing to do with—"

"Oh, don't mind me, honey. I'll love you no matter what, but I'm just worried. Things might be harder for you, sweetheart. I don't think many men are going for these women's-libber type of gals. Your dad certainly doesn't like 'em!"

Six months later Mom visited me in New York. I had just finished reading the seminal book *Our Bodies, Ourselves*. We went out to lunch, and she handed *me* a book.

"Here, Chris, *The Total Woman* by Marabel Morgan! I think it can help you, honey."

We were in a smoky restaurant on the Upper West Side near my studio apartment, which was filled with cockroaches and my other bibles, *The Feminine Mystique*, *The Diary of Anaïs Nin*, and *Sisterhood Is Powerful*. Mom patted her hair, saw the mortified look on my face, and snatched the book back to read from a quote on the book jacket.

"A Total Woman caters to her man's special quirks. . . . It teaches wives to greet their husbands at the front door wearing sexy outfits"—she paused, blushing—"like Saran wrap to cover her naked body. It's only when a woman surrenders her life to her husband, worships him, and is willing to serve him, that she becomes really beautiful to him."

"Mom, are you fucking kidding me?"

"Honey, please don't swear. I just think if you smiled a little more, it might help you find more jobs. It might even help you to find a boyfriend! You know, I've been having a rough time with Dad lately, and well, this book has given me a lot of—"

"Mom, do you not understand who I am, or at least who I'm trying to—"

"Sweetie, just read it." She leaned in and whispered, "I think you'll see that you can really get your way with men if you just treat them like kings. Don't tell your dad I told you this, but the other day I tried greeting him at the door butt naked except for a cowboy hat and high heels with a martini in hand, and my every wish was his command!"

"Oh, boy." I threw up a little in my mouth. I watched her as she talked, with a face that didn't seem to be her own anymore.

Shortly after our conversation, she told me that she'd signed up to become one of Marabel Morgan's "ambassadors," speaking at conventions, trying to sell her theories and, I guessed, also Saran wrap.

Months later, I was home for another visit. We were having a glass of wine. "So how's *The Total Woman* thing been working out for you, Mom? Are things better with Dad?"

"Oh, honey, you were right, that book turned out to be a lot of hooey. It just stopped working. After all that, I still didn't get what I wanted from him."

"Which is . . ."

"Oh, I don't know . . . It's hard to explain," she said through a weak laugh. Then out of the blue, after another cocktail, she ripped off her smile, and right in front of me, the floodgates burst open for the very first time.

"Oh, Christine, I've had it. I can't stand this anymore. Your dad's such a chauvinist!"

"Yeah, I know, Mom. So what else is new? He's always been a chauvinist."

"No, you don't understand. I think he might be having an affair."

The color instantly faded from the room. "Wait—what, Mom, really? Are you serious?"

"Well, I don't know for sure, but it just seems like he doesn't care about me anymore."

"Mom, isn't this between you and Dad?"

"I can't talk to him about anything. He doesn't listen to me. He just ridicules me!" She gasped through inconsolable sobs.

I wanted to scream at my dad, at every man. But I didn't. Instead I yelled at her.

"So fucking divorce him! Leave him! If you're that miserable, just go, Mom!" Despite the fact that I knew she would never leave him, I pressed further. "Nothing's going to change by complaining to me about it, Mom. Tell *him* about this shit, not me! Quit being such a fucking victim!"

She looked at me, stunned at the sudden loss of her one presumed ally. Then, without a word, she went back to washing the dishes.

A few days later Mom came into my room and closed the door. She sat with me on my bed.

"Chris, please, carry the banner for me."

"Carry the *banner*?" I snickered. "Mom, what do you mean? Why are you whispering?"

"Shhhh. Please just march and protest and make as much noise as possible. What you're doing is so important. Things have to change. Promise me." Her gray eyes welled up.

"Okay, sure, Mom. I promise."

"No, I mean it, honey. It's too late for me. I can't do it, but you can. The sky is the limit for you, Chris—please do it for me." She seemed smaller now, deliberately shrunken, as if not wanting to take up too much space.

I wanted to grab her and say, *It's* not *too late for you! You don't have to accept this! You are gifted and glorious and powerful! Why the fuck can't you see that?*

But I didn't say any of that. All those thoughts got caught in my throat. Instead, I just sat there, impenetrable and unforgiving as ever.

I HARDLY RECOGNIZED my mom's face in the photo that appeared in the *Detroit Free Press* sometime later. She was standing beside her still-life oil painting that won the top prize at the Detroit Art Fair. Here her smile looked different to me—effortless and earned, full of pride. Even though it was always difficult for her to sell her paintings instead of just giving them away, Mom became a gifted professional artist.

And then she decided to get a pilot's license.

"Oh, just so, you know, in case while Dad's flying our plane, he has a heart attack or something, I'll know how to get the darn thing back down." The first time she soloed, Dad and I were there. We watched as she climbed into the cockpit of the small plane alone, with her flawless hair and glistening red lipstick. Her face filled with joy as she waved and taxied down the runway. She took off, started to ascend, and then flew in circles above us. When she disappeared behind the clouds, I forgot to breathe.

IT WAS EARLY morning. My six-year-old son and I sat together at our breakfast table. I was helping him write a card for Mom, who had breast cancer now and was in the hospital.

"Here, write it with this. This is her favorite color," he said, handing me a cornflower-blue crayon.

"Okay, sweetie, and what do you want it to say?"

"Dear Grandma, I love the smile of you. From Wilson." I corrected him.

"No, honey, you mean you love her smile, right?"

"Uh-uh. Write what I said!" He put his small, warm hand on top of mine, as if to guide it.

AFTER MOM DIED, we discovered a journal tucked under a perfumed sachet in the back of a drawer. In it was a note. It read:

> *My life has been so unbelievably full. Sure, I've had a few heartbreaks but I always had faith that everything would get back on course. I think a forgiving attitude toward others, especially toward yourself, and a strong determination to keep smiling will let the sunshine in.*

I wish I hadn't spent all that time blaming her, wanting her to be different. I wish I could have told her how much her journey helped embolden mine. If only she'd gotten angry with me, stood her ground and said something like "Get off my fucking back, Christine! I'm doing the best that I can. Stop judging me so much!" But she didn't. She never would have. She especially wouldn't have said "fucking." (In our family, she might have gone to jail for that.)

Now, many years later, I understand that my son was able to see something that I couldn't. Her endless supply of smiles served her well, maybe at times as a life jacket, the only thing that kept her afloat. And maybe other times when she sensed, even for a moment, that the sky was the limit.

Dear Mom, I love the smile of you. Sorry, it just took me a while.

3

Make-Believer

THE YEAR WAS 1959. I was nine years old, sitting in a movie theater. While I waited for the monster movie *Gorgo* to begin, this sprig of a boy I hardly knew from my fourth-grade class passed me a note. Clutching my pink plastic coin purse, I opened it slowly. I read, "Santa Claus is made-up, dead and buried."

"You're a liar!" I said, wanting to snap him in two. Instead I burst into tears and, popcorn flying, bounded up the aisle.

Later that afternoon, my best friend Frannie sat with me in my room. "I don't care what anyone says, I believe in him," I confessed.

"Yeah, me too." She got up and opened her schoolbag. "But do you want to see this new lipstick I got?"

"No, Frannie, listen!" I continued. "I also know the

fairies that fly around my pillow at night are real. I can actually *feel* their wings on my face!"

"Okay, but why do their letters to you look just like your mom's handwriting?"

"So what? It's their words! And that tiny old man who puts those grains of sand into my eyes? I see his footprints in the flour that my mom leaves on the floor right next to my bed. All of these creatures exist!"

"Yeah! For sure! So anyway . . . um . . . don't you think that new guy in class, Bruce, is to die for?"

"FRANNNNIE!"

My faith in all of these magical beings stretched years past their normal expiration dates. The world of my imagination proved much more fascinating to me as a child than the world of suburban Birmingham, Michigan. But most people, as they mature, know it's idiotic, even dangerous, to be so wide-eyed. As an actor, though, being impressionable helped in my work, and so my capacity for willful naïveté only deepened.

In the summer of 1970, at a UCLA theater workshop, I was a serious student trying my hardest to pass for an unambitious hippie. But secretly eager to be a part of the acting world, I made one of my dreams almost come true.

"HEY, YOU WANT a ride? Where are you headed?" the man in the red convertible said. He was about thirty-five years old, attractive for an old man, with dark hair and yellowed, fatherly teeth. I was twenty.

After waiting an eternity at the bus stop, I'd decided to hitchhike. Hitchhiking seemed safe in 1970, and I'd just hitched around Europe with some girlfriends, so I was a pro.

"Um, I'm going to the ocean, straight down Santa Monica Boulevard." The heat radiating from his sports car warmed my bare legs.

"Well, hop in, I'm heading that way!"

"Oh, okay, thanks!" Like Blanche DuBois, I had complete faith in the kindness of strangers. So I jumped in, and we sped off.

"Hey, I'm Mack. What's your name?"

"Hi, Mack . . . Christine."

"Let me guess, you're an actress."

"How did you know? I mean, yeah, I want to be one someday."

"Oh, there's millions of you kids out here. I'm actually a producer," he said with a wide smile.

"Wow, that's so cool. What movies have you produced?"

"Oh, smaller-type movies. I doubt you've seen them."

"Oh, you mean like a John Cassavetes type?" I had taken one film class in college, History of Film 101, and heard the name.

"Yeah, Cassavetes, that's right."

"Wow, I'd love to be in movies like that someday."

"Hey, Christine, you want to go to a movie premiere with me right now?"

"Oh, wow, really, for real?"

"Yup."

"Okay, well, sure, I mean I have a couple of hours before I have to meet my friends. So yes, thank you!"

"Great, far out! My buddy who's in it said it's like . . . really good!"

"Okay, far out!" I swooned. All I knew of life was boring Michigan, and suddenly I was in a convertible on my way to a Hollywood movie premiere.

He parked the car, and we walked a couple of blocks to the "theater." I saw a tiny, dark marquee, no red carpet, no press, and no stars.

"Hey, Mack, where is everybody? Where are all the actors and the paparazzi?" I'd secretly hoped that one of my heroes, the Mouseketeer Annette Funicello or Mary Tyler Moore—the only strong female role models I'd grown up with—might be there. "Are you sure this is a premiere?" I stopped in front of the run-down building and felt countless bubbles bursting.

"Yes! We're just a little late, that's all. Come on, we can sneak in."

"Okay, but you know I really wanted to . . ."

"Come on! We're missing it!" He grabbed my arm. We opened the door and hurried into a small, musty-smelling theater, with only a handful of people inside. Mack rushed us into two worn chairs in the back row. I looked up, and there on the screen was a six-foot-tall, sixteen-foot-long dick being sucked on by the bloodred mouth of a naked woman.

My hands reflexively pulled at my short skirt. I crossed my legs twice like a pretzel. I began rethinking every choice I'd ever made in my life as I plotted how to get out of there. Then the on-screen couple started having sex . . . I thought. Never having had sex before, I couldn't be sure.

The man started whacking the naked woman on the butt so hard she began to groan and scream as if she was being mauled by a bear. *Nope, that's it, I'm absolutely positively never having sex.*

Mack kept glancing at me. He leaned over and with an unctuous grin whispered, "So what do you think? Do you like it? Is this exciting you?" He started to breathe heavily. "Hmmmm, this is making me really hard, how about you, huh? You gettin' a little wet?" He reached over in the dark, and his calloused fingers touched my thigh.

"Ugh, Jesus, no!"

I tore up the aisle as fast as I could, smashing the slimy theater doors open with such force that I almost fell out onto the street. I sprinted back to Santa Monica Boulevard and saw a bus approaching. It stopped. I jumped on. I'd never been so grateful to be on a public bus, full of nonpredatory people. Once I was safely riding toward the barely visible Pacific Ocean, I swore to myself I would never, *ever*, be so naive again.

WHEN I GRADUATED from college in 1972, I was known primarily as an accomplished and respected . . . mime. So after I'd moved to New York, and grew bored with waitressing, I believed my girlfriend Erika when she convinced me that we could make a fortune doing pantomime in Central Park. I knew it! I knew all those years of mime training would pay off! And you never know, I might finally even get an agent from this. So Erika played the clarinet while I, in whiteface, did mime. We were a terrific duo. But it was snowing and freezing, so there weren't many people that eager to see our performance. We mimed for four hours and made maybe $3.45. And we had to split it.

The next day I commiserated with my free-spirited hippie friend Patty about my mime fiasco. She then shared with me *her* fabulous part-time work idea.

"I know how you can make some money, Chris! A professional dating service. You accompany a man somewhere and get paid for it! It's totally cool. I did it last night. You get to go out to a fancy restaurant and eat a great dinner with a foreign diplomat or someone like—"

"Patty, you sure they aren't expecting more than that?"

"Chris, they're just paying for your time. Whatever happens is up to you! These guys are rich, on their own, and lonely. They just want someone to dine with. Plus you get twenty dollars."

Twenty bucks was a lot of money in 1973. "Okay, I'm in, Patty!" All dolled up in my best black dress (my only black dress), I took the subway to meet my "date" at his Park Avenue hotel. I'd never seen a hotel like this in my life. Polished marble adorned every surface.

I lifted the shiny white-and-gold rotary phone on the side table in the lobby.

"Hi, this is Christine Lahti. I'm your date for the evening. I'm here."

"Hello, Christine. Come up!"

"No, actually I'd prefer it if you came down."

I knew enough not to go alone to a strange man's hotel room. Besides, I wasn't about to miss out on dinner at a five-star restaurant. I'd already played out the fantasy. We would speak French together over an expensive bottle of wine, in an amber-lit room with a panoramic view of Manhattan. Having been an avid fan of the Miss America pageants growing up, it's possible, in this fantasy, I was even wearing a crown.

"I understand completely, Christine, but I'm expecting an important long-distance business call. I'm sure he'll call within the next twenty minutes. Why don't you come up, we'll have a quick glass of champagne, and then we can go right out."

"Okay," I agreed, still wary.

My ears popped as I took the elevator up to an impossibly high floor. I walked slowly down the long, elegant hallway with its thick white carpet, and knocked on the door.

"So nice to meet you, Christine! I'm Michael. Please, come in."

Dressed in a stylish suit and tie, my date seemed polite and gracious. He looked about forty years old, had thick black hair, and stood at least a head shorter than me, even though I purposely wore flats. I instinctively slumped a little.

"Please sit down! Would you like a glass of champagne?"

Soft beiges and creamy whites drenched the spacious room. I'd rarely been in a place like this that didn't have plastic covering the furniture. While sipping our Dom Perignon, we discussed politics, his brilliant career, and my promising career. Patty was right—he just wanted some company! This felt completely legit and fantastic. Twenty minutes went by, then thirty, then a whole hour. The call never came.

"Hey, Michael, why don't we go to dinner now? I'm getting really hungry."

"I'm so sorry. I don't know why he is so late!"

"Well, your friend is pretty darn rude, keeping you waiting like this." I emptied my crystal tulip champagne glass.

"I couldn't agree more." He refilled my glass with the rest of the bottle.

"Fine, can we at least order room service?"

He dialed, ordered filet mignons and a bottle of cabernet, and hung up the phone.

"Hey, Michael," I said, "parlez-vous français?"

"No, why do you ask?"

"Nothing—I just wondered." I smiled as I sank back into the plush couch. He sat down next to me. I noticed his girlie-smelling cologne for the first time.

"I want to know more about Christine. What's it like in . . . the Midwest?" he inquired, as though he was asking about Disneyland.

"Ohhh, well, it's beautiful, lots of lakes. It's called the Water and Winter Wonderland," I added proudly.

"Really? Isn't that fascinating! So tell me, what's a nice girl like you doing in a job like this?"

"Yeah, right . . . wait, what do you mean?"

"Come on, you know what I mean. This is an *escort* service." He put his arm around me.

My proper Lutheran upbringing flashed before my eyes. Oh dear God, where did he get that I was a . . . *I'm going to kill you, Patty!*

"Oh boy. There's been a huge misunderstanding here,

Michael. My friend told me that . . . this was just a . . . uh, never mind." I grabbed my purse and coat. "I have to, uh . . . I have to go."

"No, wait, don't." He inched even closer; I sprinted to the door. He glared at me and reached into his pocket.

Oh my fucking God, is he going for his gun? Am I about to be raped at gunpoint, or murdered? I ran to escape and opened the door to the . . . bathroom. Shit. I slammed the door. I locked it. Oh God, what should I do? My heart was beating out of my dress. He started to knock on the door.

"Please just let me go!" I begged him. "I'm really sorry, I didn't know what this job was! I'm not a hooker!"

"It's okay, Christine, you can leave. Just come out of the bathroom." Finally, I emerged, armed with the toilet plunger. He reached into his pocket again.

"No, please don't shoot!"

"Jesus Christ, calm down! I'm just getting out my wallet to pay you your twenty bucks!"

But the drama queen in me knew better. I flew past him, through the correct door, and down the hall so fast my feet barely touched the carpet. Even though I was an agnostic, I prayed, *Oh, Jesus, God, Lord, Savior, whatever your name is . . . if I can just please get down this elevator alive, I'll believe, I'll . . . believe!*

When I got down to the lobby, I rushed to the public phone. As I waited for Patty to pick up, I noticed my image reflected in the marble. I saw an awkwardly lanky young woman, huddled over the phone, with wet stains under the arms of her cheap rayon dress.

No one answered. I hung up. It probably wasn't even a

big deal to my "free love" friend Patty. Or maybe she just had a tendency to believe, the way I did.

I'm aware that being so adept at the art of make-believing has also had its benefits. Later in life, this skill would help me to stand on a bare wooden stage and imagine I lived in a castle in Elizabethan England. Or on a plantation in the Deep South. It would help me to become a Hungarian Holocaust survivor. A spinster southern belle. My ability to immerse myself in imaginary circumstances has enabled me to get inside the skin of a whole variety of characters and make a good living while doing it.

Thankfully, over time, I've discovered that the suspension of disbelief is different, and a lot less dangerous, than naïveté. But in that moment I was just a gullible young woman with stars in her eyes and sweaty armpits who desperately wanted to believe she was so much more than just someone's escort.

I buttoned up my wool green coat. I walked out of the fancy hotel. And on the packed subway ride home, I couldn't stop thinking about how nice those twenty dollars would have been. I picked at the tiny run in my $2.95 panty hose, a run that soon would become a fleshy four-lane highway down my entire leg.

4

Hidden

EVEN BACK THEN, when I was twelve, it didn't look all that special—just a flurry of high weeds on the bluff near the road. The grass was flattened by my sprouting bean-pole body huddling there—as if a deer had slept on it. The air was thick with dazed insects barely able to move in the Michigan summer. The only sounds were the screeching of cicadas and the occasional whoosh of a speeding car going by. At least I could see the lake from my hiding place. On the rare sunny days, it was a slash of turquoise, but usually the water was as flat gray as the sky. The spot was only minutes from our summer cottage in Bellaire, Michigan, but it felt like miles. It took me forever to get there through the tangled undergrowth. But none of that mattered: what was important was that when I was there, nestled in among the brambles and wildflowers, nobody could see me.

Privacy was at a premium in our cottage. My three sisters and I shared one small bedroom. The slanting ceiling of the A-frame forced us to walk hunched over like preteen grandmothers. We were separated from our brothers' room by a thin knotty-pine wall that rose only three-quarters of the way to the ceiling. At any time, day or night, their devilish eyes could be seen peeking over that wall. This secluded hilltop spot became my secret refuge where I could go to get away from all of them—and, most importantly, to be sad.

Sadness was not well tolerated by my family; my parents simply didn't believe in it. Growing up, I watched as they drank "Torch Lake Specials"—lemonade, whiskey, blue curaçao, and maraschino cherries—every night to wash away any trace of theirs. In our family you were expected to be happy. Being quiet was acceptable, too, but if you were downhearted, you were to go to your room and wait it out.

On the wall behind my sisters' and my two double beds were our role models: four framed faces of the beatific girls featured on the packages of Quilted Northern toilet paper. They were all doe-eyed, smiling, each holding a blanket, a bunny, a kitten, or a bouquet of pansies up to her painted pink cheek. Each sister had the picture of the girl she most resembled above her side of the bed. My doppelgänger had long brown hair and hazel eyes, just like me. They served as a kind of not-so-subtle reminder that it was our duty to be just like them.

IN MY LAKESIDE sanctuary, there was no pressure to emulate one of those toilet-tissue cherubs, squeezably soft and pliable. Instead, I got to just sit in whatever I was feeling and savor it, as rich and sweet as caramel.

In *Housekeeping*, a movie based on Marilynne Robinson's novel in which I played the character Sylvie, there was a scene where she was confronted by a gaggle of town ladies concerned that Sylvie's nieces looked sad. She responded sharply, "Of course they're sad. They've lost their mother. They should be sad!" The ladies looked at Sylvie like she should have been locked up. I always thought about that scene whenever I remembered how uncomfortable sadness was for our family, as unwelcome as a drunk uncle showing up uninvited at Thanksgiving.

I first felt the exquisite snag of a broken heart while sitting alone and quiet in my refuge. It was also where I first cupped my hand over my breast and noticed how, quite suddenly, my body was different. I was there when I practiced kissing on my forearm, with my eyes opened and then closed, with tongue, then without. That spot held the secrets of my big plans about how I'd someday fully escape from the chaos of my family.

No one ever knew about my secluded place until almost fifty years later when I returned, excited to share it with my husband. It seemed so silly—almost embarrassing—as I pointed it out to him. The trees across the road were so mature that there was practically no view of the lake. The weeds looked shorter, like no one could have ever been concealed by them. The once flattened grass stood straight and tall. The hill seemed barely a hill at all, more like a small bump in the flat terrain. The road had become a highway, its traffic noises louder, more constant. There was no trace of the hidden girl who sat alone there. Her secrets, as exposed as her former hiding place, had long since vanished.

The wind bent the tops of the birches, revealing the lake at its most heart-stopping blue. I sat here with my partner of nearly thirty years, neither of us talking; gratefully visible now, in this ordinary place, just a stone's throw away from our family's cottage on the lake.

5

Walking

I T WAS A crisp autumn morning in New York City in 1973. As a twenty-three-year-old hippie-meets-serious-actress-wannabe, I knew that doing a television commercial was beneath me. However, my most lucrative acting job to date had been an off-off-off-off-Broadway play that paid in subway tokens, and being a waitress had lost a lot of its bohemian allure. After pounding the pavement for almost two years, still without an agent, I was thinking I could probably handle a *little* selling out.

So I prepared to go to an open audition for two national commercials. I reluctantly parted with my beloved armpit and leg hair. I threw on some dime-store makeup and packed myself into the rush-hour uptown subway. I met with the casting director, John Anderson—middle-aged, disheveled, and hair-challenged, but he seemed professional and polite. We talked briefly. He took a few pictures. I left.

Two days later he called me and asked me to come back in for a callback! I'd received feedback that I needed to look more conventional, so I hot-rollered and Aqua-Netted my frizzy hair into a large sticky helmet. I put on my polyester three-piece suit, which had the texture of a car tire. I glanced in my cracked antique mirror and decided I looked like Tammy Faye. But I sucked in my gut, yanked up my control-top panty hose, slipped on my height-minimizing flats, and headed out to change the course of my life.

I arrived at Mr. Anderson's office on Seventy-Fifth Street and Lexington twenty minutes early. He swung the door open.

"Christine Lahti! Come on in, sweetheart. This is your lucky day. Guess what? You got the gigs!"

At first I thought he'd mixed me up with someone else. I stood there, skinless. "What? Really? Are you sure?"

"I'm sure," he said, smiling.

"But how? I mean, thank you so much, Mr. Anderson, but I haven't even auditioned for them yet!"

"John, call me John, come in!" He let me into his reception area. "So . . . I showed your pictures to these two director friends of mine, and you're just the type they are looking for!"

A weight suddenly lifted from my chest. I was going to finally be a professional actress! And two national commercials—that could pay my rent for years. I could quit my fucking waitress job!

"Really, Mr. Ander— I mean, John? You have no idea what this means to me!" I asked him if he wanted me to read.

"Oh, no, you don't have to audition, the commercials are already yours!"

I couldn't believe it. I crossed all my fingers inside my pockets as he took my arm and walked me into his inner office. He sat down at his cluttered desk, picked up a used tissue, and wiped his forehead with it.

"Have a seat, Christine." He leaned back in his chair. "First of all, you should know you stand to make at least ten grand a piece on these, and with residuals . . ."

I stopped listening and instantly pictured my new cockroach-free apartment with its separate bedroom and window air-conditioning unit.

"Holy shit! I mean . . . sorry, John, but this is so incredible! So when do I . . ."

He shuffled some papers on his desk as he said, "Well, it's really quite simple, Christine. All you have to do first is have sex with the directors."

I froze. I was sure I misheard him, or that he was joking. He must have been joking. I laughed.

John didn't laugh back.

"Wait, what?" I asked. "I'm sorry . . . What are you saying?" I had heard about the Hollywood casting couch for movies. But this was New York City. For two *breakfast cereal* commercials!

He looked at me, amused. "Look, sweetheart, this is just the way it's done. You said you've got no connections in show biz, right? But hey, if you don't really care that much about being an actress—"

"No! I do! More than anything in the world, but—"

"Look, it's no big deal, everybody does it. Dunaway,

Fonda, Collins . . . all of 'em. It's just a reality for someone like you, sweetheart." He chuckled, as if he couldn't believe anyone could be so naive.

I sank lower in my cold metal chair.

"Look, let's face it, Christine." He gazed at the curvature of my nose. "You're . . . uh . . . well, an unconventional type. And what are you, almost six feet tall?" He said it as if accusing me of murdering both my parents. "Well, how the hell else do you think you're going to make it?"

"I don't know . . . I thought . . . that I was . . ."

"Let me guess, talented and a hard worker? Or do you think you're going to make it on your looks?"

"No . . . no, of course not . . . but I just . . . I thought you said I . . . I mean, how could you think that I would ever . . . I mean . . . I . . . I . . . I . . ." I started crying and couldn't seem to stop, so I grabbed my headshot and tore out of his office. As I pummeled the elevator button in the hallway, I heard him yelling through his door, "Hey, Christine, you're a fool if you think you're going to make it any other way!"

The elevator hurled me down to the lobby. The revolving glass door spat me out into the street. I felt lightheaded. I just wanted to go home, but where was I? What street was this? A cab went by—no, I couldn't afford that. Besides, I still couldn't quit bawling. So I began the seventy-five-block trek back to my apartment.

I started heading down Lexington Avenue. When I got to Seventy-Second Street, tears dribbling down my non-absorbent jacket, I could barely see where I was going. An assault of fire engines and ambulances went by, and over their sirens, I started talking out loud to myself like a lunatic. "Oh God," I gasped between sobs. "What if he's right? Does this mean I'll never get to be an actress?" A woman walking next to me with her baby stroller noticed and suddenly pulled away. "What the fuck you looking at, lady?" I barked at her.

As she darted across the street, I heard *smooch, smooch* and a piercing whistle. I looked up and a construction worker called out, "Hey, pretty girl come here, I wanna lick you." *Jesus.* I picked up my pace. "Hey, where ya goin', hot stuff? Smile! Whassa matter—you can't smile?" Smile? What was he talking about? But sure enough, as I lowered my head, I found my face contorting into a kind of automatic grimace.

Then at Sixty-Third Street, I realized that I was still carrying my pathetic headshot. I looked down at it. When the hell did I become my mom? The made-up face, the perfect hair, the phony smile. This was the way she always looked, even when my dad, all of us, made fun of her, laughing at her opinions, about . . . everything.

As my tears fell into little glossy puddles on the eight-by-ten, I stared at my image. No wonder I can't get an agent, I thought. I had hideously small ferret eyes, my nose was way too wide at the top, and it actually hooked to the left at the tip. I looked like a man in drag. And I was too fucking tall! What was I thinking? Forget "unconventional." Everything about me was just . . . wrong.

At Fifty-Seventh Street, I headed west and saw Carnegie Hall. My heart still pounding, I wasn't sure I'd ever get home. A tall, confident-looking young woman with a briefcase walked by me and for some reason laughed. Was she laughing at me? At the four layers of mascara that had run down my splotchy red cheeks? When I left my apartment this morning I felt like her. Or maybe I just thought I did.

My dad's advice from when I was in high school suddenly echoed in my ears again. *Why buy the cow, Chris, if you can get the milk for free?* It wasn't until that instant that I truly understood my girl-value. I wish I'd said "Well, Dad, why buy a whole pig, just to get a little sausage?" But I didn't. I just shut up and went back out to pasture.

Somewhere near Forty-Eighth Street, a silver-haired businessman walked by and perused my body like it was an item on his à la carte dinner menu. I instantly pictured the silver-haired professional actor Chester Martin, and that memorable night when he offered me some of *his* sage career advice: "Look, Christine, you have absolutely no light to shed upon the human existence. Your desire to be an actress is a pipe dream, I'm afraid. You have no hope of making it as a professional."

He was from Nebraska, although his accent was distinctly British. I considered for a second that he was saying this only because I hadn't let him fuck me the previous night. But then I decided that no, he was simply being brutally honest.

Close to Times Square now, the fumes from Papaya King pulled me in. I decided to drown my sorrows in a super-duper-deluxe hot dog. As I stuffed the tube of meat paste with its permissible percentage of pig snouts and 480 milligrams of salt into my mouth, I looked up. All I could see were gigantic billboards of nearly naked women with bodies that would have made a Barbie doll jealous. They all looked like they were having sex with Mercedeses, Marlboros, and bottles of Johnnie Walker Red. Then I noticed a flood of men pouring out of the towering office buildings and a stream of women trickling out behind them. I thought of college, of all the marches for civil rights and equality, when out of sheer habit, we girls marched *behind* the men. We made the peanut butter and jelly sandwiches, and they made all the speeches. I even turned down directing a play in college because I wasn't comfortable telling boys what to do.

Near Twenty-Fifth Street, the cold breeze stinging my wet face, someone walked by me with a boom box blaring Johnny Mathis: "*Look at me, I'm as helpless as a kitten up a tree. . . .*" As I dodged the crush of people on the sidewalk, my mind went back to fifth grade. I remembered slow dancing on the shag carpet in Frannie Martin's basement with my boyfriend, the freckle-faced Steve Mathews. He was only six inches shorter than me. The boys called me the Jolly Green Giant, and I knew one thing for sure: that being tall was bad. Johnny Mathis crooned from the hi-fi while we swayed: "*. . . and I feel like I'm clinging to a cloud. I can't understand—I get misty just holding your hand.*"

I knew this was going to be a boy-girl party, but I had no idea it was actually a *make-out* party. Steve started leading me toward the pitch-black kissing room. We found the only available chair. He sat me on his bird lap. Everywhere I looked were the shadows of other couples kissing, groping, and moaning. I certainly wasn't getting misty holding

Steve's hand. As I saw his mouth moving in, closer and closer, I thought, Oh God, what do I do? Saying no just wasn't an option, so thinking fast, I cupped his hot pink ear and whispered as softly as I could, "Hey, Steve? I'm really sorry, but is it okay if we just sort of make the sounds instead of really kissing? Can we just pretend, is that okay? Please?"

"Oh, okay, I guess," answered Steve, surprised and more than a little disappointed.

So, lips miles apart, we fake made out. *Mmmm, smooch, smooch, ahhhhh, ssssmooch, mmmmm.*

I glanced around the dark room to make sure we'd gotten away with it. I leaned in close again. "Okay, thank you, Steve! That wasn't so bad, right?"

That freckle-faced fucker broke up with me the next day.

Horns were now blaring in the bumper-to-bumper traffic. A jackhammer rattled my brain. I passed by a playground. I heard a little girl, about eight years old, yelling. She was on top of a jungle gym, a sea of little boys beneath her. "I'm the king of the castle and you're the dirty rascals! Na, na, na, na, na!" she sang. I couldn't take my eyes off her. She noticed my staring, so I walked away. She reminded me of when I was that age, a fearless pixie-haired tomboy, before the world tried to suck the sass out of me. I was called bossy growing up, but in my family that meant bratty and selfish. If my brothers were called bossy, that meant they were leaders and should, of course, become president—a double standard that would render me phobic about being a leader later in life, and leave me sans sass when I needed it most, like back in that casting director's office.

I started to head even farther west once I hit Eighteenth Street. The wind from the Hudson River whipped around the buildings. A light rain started to fall. Soon I found myself passing through a forest of hookers in impossibly short skirts. One brunette with long curls tried to wave down willing cars. A couple of teenage boys walked past, giggling and pointing at her. She simply sighed and regarded them calmly, her thick lipstick cracking from the cold.

"Oh, you poor boys, you just ain't on my agenda today," she scoffed as she moved on, shoulders back, her head held high. I kept glancing back at her. As I walked, I found myself imitating her proud posture, her long, purposeful strides.

I finally reached my building in the West Village. I heard "Stop it! No, goddamn it!" A woman was yelling across the street. I saw a man hitting her in front of a bar.

Without hesitating, I shouted, "Hey! Leave her alone, shithead! Stop it! Get your hands off her, or I'm calling the cops!"

Startled, the man released her. Then the woman took a few steps toward me and yelled, "Mind your own fucking business, bitch!"

I fumbled with my keys, trying to unlock my front door. Finally inside, I sprinted up the four flights of stairs, two steps at a time, to my apartment. I threw open my door, bolted it twice behind me, and leaned up against it, trying to catch my breath. As I disassembled my damp Tammy Faye costume, kicking the jacket and vest across the floor, flinging my flats, and wiggling out of my girdle panty hose, I started talking to myself again.

"I'm DONE. I am never letting anyone treat me like that again. And fuck anyone who tries, because none of you are going to be on MY fucking agenda ever again! And guess what, you casting director prick! I don't give a shit what you think—" I crushed the girdle stockings into a ball, hurling them into the trash can. "I'm going to be a successful, RESPECTED actress, you pathetic loser! And fuck you, Chester Martin! You want me to shed some light? Well, how about the lights on BROADWAY, you pretentious asshole! Hey, you piece-of-shit construction worker, SMILING IS NOT . . . MY FUCKING . . . GIRL-DUTY!" I seized a tissue from my kitchen counter and rubbed off the remnants of my makeup. "And I'm not stopping, goddamn it, until ALL women are treated equally!" I bent over and shook out my hair. "AHHHH! SO MAKE WAY FOR ALL OF US MOTHERFUCKERS BECAUSE HERE WE . . ."

The phone rang. "Hello, who's this?" I asked, hoping I didn't sound as winded as I felt. It was a boy I'd been praying for weeks would call me. He was an artist and he was kind and made me laugh. He said he knew it was last-minute, but would I like to go to a big movie premiere with him that evening? Nearly shrieking with excitement, I said, "Oh my God, I'd love to! Thanks!"

I tossed the phone onto a chair. Tearing off my slip, I dashed into the bathroom for a quick shower, but as I looked in the broken mirror, I noticed my red, bloated eyes and remembered that super-duper-deluxe high-sodium hot dog I'd just eaten. "Oh shit. Plus look at my fucking stomach. I've gained at least five pounds in the last week." I marched straight back to the phone.

I stopped mid-march.

"Wait, Jesus Christ, what is wrong with you? You look good enough! What was that seventy-five-block walk for anyway? Did you learn nothing?"

I glanced back in the mirror again. I picked up the phone.

"Oh, hi, Bruce, listen, I'm *so* sorry, but I totally forgot, I made plans with my sister tonight," I lied.

I hung up and sank down onto my extra-long twin bed. I wrapped myself in my tattered, patchwork quilt. After a few minutes, I emerged. I slowly stood up, and with my long-legged strides, walked over to my soot-covered window. With all my strength, I pried it open, then gazed up at the brightly lit New York City night sky. I closed my eyes and took a long, deep breath.

I'll take another walk tomorrow.

6

Shit Happens

OH MY GOD, where's the crutch, where's the crutch? I'm onstage in front of a thousand people and . . . I CAN'T FIND THE FUCKING CRUTCH! We're at the climax of act one in *Cat on a Hot Tin Roof,* and I am a consummate professional, so there's no wiggle room for this kind of fuck-up.

I'm at the Long Wharf Theatre in New Haven in 1985, performing my first leading role in one of the classics. As scripted, the actor playing my husband, Brick, throws his crutch across the room at me while I duck behind the bed. I'm supposed to then pick it up off the floor and bring it back to him. But tonight I can't find the damn thing!

The dialogue goes something like:

"Brick, I'm not good . . . but I'm honest! Give me credit for just that, will you *please*? . . . But Brick?

Skipper is dead! I'm alive! Maggie the Cat is alive! I am alive, alive! I am . . ."

[*Brick then hurls the crutch at her, across the bed she took refuge behind, and pitches forward onto the floor as she completes her speech.*]

"—alive!"

The rest of the scene is entirely dependent on my returning the crutch to him so he can stand up again. As I'm flop-sweating, frantically scanning the entire stage for the crutch, I think . . . Okay, maybe I should just improvise something like "Oh, Brick, I know you just tried to kill me with your crutch, but if you love me, even the tiniest little bit, I know you would HELP ME TO FIND IT!"

But no, I can't say that. So what should I do? I look out into the audience, and right away see the crutch leaning on a woman's seat in the front row. Jesus, Brick's got shitty aim, I think. I have no other options, so I climb down off the stage—in character—into the dark theater and sashay up to the woman. I reach for the crutch and try to take it, but . . . she's grabbing it back! Are you kidding me?

So I pull it again, and she pulls it back. I pull . . . and she pulls it back harder. *Please, please,* PLEASE *lady, just give me back my fucking prop!* With the entire audience now laughing, I yank it as hard as I can. Suddenly I look down in the dark and notice that the crutch-stealer has a large cast on her extended leg.

Oh God, this is *her* freakin' crutch?! I hand the crutch back to the lady, shrug, and mumble in my Maggie accent something like "Oh, I . . . I didn't need that anyway." I climb back onto the stage, only to see Brick's crutch embedded in some fish netting on the wall behind the bed. The audience is now howling so loudly, the theater might explode. I have no choice but to continue with the dialogue as written, shouting to be heard.

"Brick, I've been to a doctor in Memphis. A—a gynecologist. I've been completely examined and there is no reason why we can't have a child whenever we want to. Are you listening to me? Are you? Are you LISTENING TO ME!"

"Yes. I hear you, Maggie. But how the hell on earth do you imagine—that you're going to have a child by a man who can't stand you?"

The laughter builds as my theater career comes to a screeching halt.

I rescue the camouflaged crutch and hand it back to my costar. He's finally able to pull himself up from the floor. We finish the scene. The curtain comes down, and the actor playing Brick, who's been looking away from me this whole time, says "Holy shit! The audience is going crazy! What did I do that was so fucking funny?"

I just can't find the words.

BEING RAISED IN a dysfunctional family with six kids, we all had to figure out our own way to stand out from the crowd. I saw an old home video recently where I elbowed my older sister out of the way when we were performing "Honey Bun" from *South Pacific* for our parents. My mom once told me that if any of my siblings sang too loudly, threatening to drown me out, I'd simply put my hands over their mouths.

When I was growing up, my dad would dole out his disappointment in us as readily as he handed us our weekly allowances. The fear of engendering this disappointment drove me to shine in all that I did. For instance, Dad would give us the nightly challenge of being members of the "clean plate club" at dinner. We had to eat everything on our plates because there were "starving children in China." What I was starving for was my dad's approval, so I not only devoured every morsel, I would lick my plate so clean that it sparkled with my saliva.

Standing out didn't stop there. It carried over into adolescence and then adulthood, with awards and trophies becoming important measures of that success. For me, growing up female, there weren't a lot of opportunities for prizes in sports, so I became obsessed with Girl Scout badges. At summer camp I always coveted the Best Camper ribbons, not only winning "cleanest cabin" but sucking up to every single one of the counselors. In grade school I once got a bad-conduct check mark on my report card for talking too much in class. It felt like I'd been caught setting the school on fire.

Then I discovered theater. Yes, I cherished being able to play different characters, but what other job validates you with hundreds of people standing, cheering, and applauding when you finish your day's work? I was hooked! But as I went on to study acting in New York City, whenever my work was criticized at all, I felt like a failure. I remember one teacher asking me, "Why are you taking a class if you're so afraid of making mistakes?" Even as I began working professionally, I had to be perfect.

My need for perfection was a drive to be not just a model "artiste" but an ultimate feminist as well. I felt a responsibility to be accountable, to put only positive, three-dimensional images of women out into the world. I became so hard-core about this that my agents started to get worried. Many of the "good" parts in film and on television in those days were demeaning to women. I refused to even have a meeting for the female lead in a movie that went on to become a massive international hit. "I won't be able to sleep at night if I play that two-dimensional, misogynistic part," I self-righteously told my bewildered, male agent. God forbid anyone should ever judge *me* for "selling out."

But there came a point when I was getting weary of all the waitressing, and I got a commercial for . . . Joy dishwashing liquid. Oh fuck. There were many sleepless nights over that one. I finally rationalized that it would be okay to do because at least I'd be portraying a housewife who was *also* the coach for her son's softball team. I still had to have an orgasm as I stared at a gleaming plate, saying "Hey, I can see myself!" But at least I got to wear sweats and a baseball cap. In the years that followed, I became much more forgiving of myself whenever I had to choose certain roles just to pay the bills.

IN 2008 I was nominated for a Golden Globe Award. On the day of the ceremony, my beauty SWAT team had just departed my bathroom. Dressed in a borrowed Hervé Léger gown that fit like a glamorous girdle, I sat down to put the finishing touches on my speech. I'd been nominated a lot. I'd won once, a long time ago so it was past time for another trophy fix. I knew people made fun of the Golden Globes, but to me they were the equivalent of a Nobel Peace Prize.

I practiced giving my speech, over and over. It had to be self-deprecating, with just the right amount of gratitude and humility. After a few run-throughs, I folded it neatly into a square and stuffed it into my purse, knowing deep down that the speech would likely end up in my "grave-yard drawer," where all my dried-up lipsticks and unused speeches went to die.

Once at the Golden Globes, with all of the fancy film people near the front and all of us inferior TV people way back in television Siberia, I perused the lineup in the program. I saw that my category was toward the very end of what I knew was an endless show. It was hard to sit still. I felt too nervous to eat. My dress was already too tight anyway. I didn't dare take even a sip of wine until after my category. So, sucking in my stomach, I decided to get up to go to the ladies' room with my girlfriend for a quick touch-up. I reapplied my lip gloss for the fourth time in front of the brightly lit mirror. But while I waited for my friend to pee, an uneasy feeling came over me.

"Kathy, uh, I'm gonna go back, I'll see you in there, okay?"

"Okay, sure, honey!" she yelled out over the sound of the toilets flushing.

Walking toward the ballroom, I was pulling up my bra

straps to even out my cleavage when a woman heading toward the restroom stopped me. "Oh my God, hey, you just won!"

"Ha ha, yeah, right." And I'm thinking, What a terrible joke, lady. That's not even remotely funny!

"No, really, you did! You just won for Best Actress in a TV Drama."

"But that's impossible! My category is at the very end!"

"Well, sorry, but you just missed it."

Are you fucking kidding me? Goddamn it! I rushed in to see Robin Williams vamping on the stage. Before Robin got onstage, the producer of *Chicago Hope* had apparently walked up and announced, "Christine, where are you? I know you want this. I knew when I looked over and saw she wasn't there, it was because she's in the ladies' room . . ." Then Robin Williams had climbed up and started improvising to keep the show from moving on.

I scrambled down through the tables like a madwoman. But during those one hundred or so hurried steps, something changed. I felt like I was floating, lighter somehow, like I was finally loosened from a straitjacket. The worst thing that could have happened, happened. And it was fine. All the years of striving for perfection, all that panic— about lost props, about conduct marks on report cards, about selling out—got left on the bathroom floor of the Century Plaza Hotel.

Onstage, I noticed that the sea of faces before me all seemed freshly awakened from a snooze—giddy, slap-happy, drunk. I grabbed Robin Williams's dinner napkin out of his hands. Without thinking, I started wiping my hands with it. I approached the mike and said the first words that came to me: "Sorry, Mom, but I was in the bathroom." I tried to read my prepared speech, but I couldn't. Every planned, scripted word seemed contrived and stale. After waving to a few friends, I thanked a bunch of people and then just started laughing. I even forgot to suck in my stomach.

When I got back to my table and a *giant* glass of wine, I picked up my program and finally noticed the asterisk: *Order of Awards to Be Presented—Subject to Mother-fucking Change.

People still stop me a lot in airports and at Starbucks to say, "Wait, don't I know you from somewhere?" As I'm about to proudly run down the list of my latest films and trophies, they interrupt: "No, wait! I know! You were the woman in the bathroom at that award show!"

I'm fairly confident that when I die, although I will have left behind a whole body of work as a serious actor and a director, there will be only one thing written on my tombstone:

CHRISTINE LAHTI—

SHE WAS IN THE BATHROOM

WHEN SHE WON HER GOLDEN GLOBE

Hey, shit happens.

7

The Wet Towel

I MAGINE MY HORROR as I looked down and saw it, splayed across my summer-weight goose-down comforter . . . on *my* side of the bed. Dumped into a sodden heap, without any regard to the fresh linen beneath it. Indifferent to the person who would now have to sleep on clammy sheets. Long forgotten, it simply waited for someone else to pick it up: his chauvinist pig of a wet towel.

This boyfriend and I had been dating for a couple of years when he moved into my newly purchased, architecturally challenged one-bedroom condo on West Seventy-First Street. We'd decided to take this terror-inducing "next step" because, up until this towel assault, it had been pretty smooth sailing. My therapist had encouraged me. "Why not?" she said. "Think of it as a laboratory experiment!"

Well, he might as well have just lifted his leg and peed

on my bed, marking it like a dog. No matter how much discussion we'd had about equality, somewhere, deep down, my new roommate expected me to be his "wife." Talk is cheap, I thought, staring at the gray puddle spreading on my beloved quilt; the proof is in the . . . towel.

Tommy knew how gun-shy I was about commitment. I'd shared with him the cautionary tales of past boyfriends who seemed to require that I make myself smaller so they wouldn't feel threatened. Like that underemployed actor who would fly into a purple rage anytime I had any career success. Or that withholding, domineering blond musician with the wire-rimmed glasses, a doppelgänger of my dad.

Tommy had heard plenty about my pervasively sexist upbringing. How my mom had to surrender her entire identity when she agreed to marry my father. He'd even witnessed it firsthand.

On a visit home, Tommy watched how she'd wait on Dad, hand and foot, as he sat for hours in front of the television watching sports. Through the din of cheering and the drone of Howard Cosell, Tommy could hear Mom cheerfully ask, "Excuse me, Ted, can I get cha anything, honey? Would ja like some more . . ."

"Sshhh!" interrupted Dad, urgently holding up his index finger. "GO BLUE! YES . . . TOUCHDOWN!!"

She'd wait patiently for the play to be over, feigning interest in the pileup of beefy athletes on the screen as she smoothed her helmetlike hair.

"Now, what is it you wanted?" he'd finally respond, in a voice mildly tinged with annoyance.

"Oh, sorry! Um . . . I just wondered if I could bring you another beer or something else . . . maybe a Reuben?"

"You're an angel in disguise!" he'd whisper distractedly, his eyes fixed on the endless series of instant replays.

Her made-up face fixed in a smile, she'd empty his ashtray, restock his peanuts-and-red-hots mix, bring him a fresh Budweiser and an expertly grilled sauerkraut and corned beef sandwich. She was careful not to get in his sight line as she quietly set up his TV table and placed his napkin on his madras plaid trousers.

"Holy shit. What was *that*?" Tommy said to me later that night in Dad's wood-paneled den on the pull-out leather couch. Even though we were living together, both thirty-two years old, we had to sleep in separate beds at my parents' house because we weren't married.

"I felt like I was on Mars," he went on.

"Yeah, well, welcome to my world," I agreed, embarrassed.

He laughed. "No wonder you're so fucked-up!"

I looked at him sadly.

"No, no, no," he replied, dancing as fast as he could. "I meant . . . no wonder you're so paranoid. Look, sweetheart, I promise you, that guy in there with the madras pants and red hots? I will never, ever, be anything remotely like him."

Although clearly supportive of women's rights, Tommy didn't exactly call himself a feminist yet. But back then, any man who identified as such just seemed like he was trying to get laid. At the time, I accepted his preferred word: "humanist." He swore that he loved me *because* I had big dreams, and that he shared my need for independence.

But then . . . he played the fucking wet-towel card, knowing full well that my hair-trigger trust was at stake. Was this blatant disrespect a sign of something even deeper? Was he actually saying, in the most passive-aggressive way possible, that he wanted out? Fuck, I should have known. I'd had misgivings from the start.

"SO . . . I MET this guy . . . Tommy," I'd told my shrink a few years prior, when I was thirty-two.

She lifted her eyebrows. "And?"

"I don't know. He's just so . . . *nice.*"

"Jesus, Christine," she said, looking at me sadly. Her voice became husky. "What makes you think you don't deserve to be with someone who's nice?"

Okay. Shit. She had a point. She knew that the only men I felt comfortable with at that point were gay. And here was this funny, sexy, seemingly nonsexist heterosexual man who could do magic tricks, named Tommy Schlamme. Eventually, with her help, taking baby steps, I began to understand the attractive and essential nature of kindness.

Tommy and I became friends first, and then gradually lovers. Although I kept denying others' insistence that I was falling in love, something strange and wonderful was happening; a kind of tender trust. After he'd moved in and I confronted him about the towel debacle, he apologized, reassuring me it wasn't a sign of anything except carelessness. I also found out that we shared many of the same issues; neither of us had any interest in the limitations of traditional gender roles. Yikes. Could this guy actually be a potential life partner?

Note that I said "life partner." Marriage wasn't even on my radar back then. I knew, as Gloria Steinem said, that marriage would seem like the last choice I would ever have. Why would any sane female voluntarily choose to enter that kind of prison? A woman's wedding day was touted as being the greatest day of her life, when really it was the last day of *her* life. Everyone stands and applauds her as she walks down the aisle with her father, who then transfers his property to her soon-to-be husband. The marriage license was nothing more than a deed of ownership.

Yet against all odds, despite my trepidation, our "experiment" worked. And several years later, we decided to wed. We were planning to start a family soon, and we thought it might be better for our future kids if we got married. Plus, we liked the idea of a big dance party. This miracle occurred on September 4, 1983, at the Dairy in the middle of Central Park, officiated by a dour woman from the New York Society for Ethical Culture. We had handwritten our humorless ceremony, battling over every word. I felt especially adamant that there be no hint of any patriarchal religious bullshit. Our one expression of spirituality was a reading from *The Color Purple* in which the character Shug describes God, who could be seen in the color purple, as "not a He or a She but an 'It.'" Speaking our no-nonsense vows to each other, Tommy and I both knew we were heading into uncharted territory. We figured we'd just have to make up our own rules as we went along.

We went on to raise three children. Not terribly unconventionally, except we tried our best to do it together, as partners, with as much levity as humanly possible. It's still been important to me to maintain separate bank accounts, though we share all our expenses as equally as we can. Certainly not without many extreme ups and downs, and maybe partly because we've spent a lot of time apart, we are now going on *thirty-four years*. Though a friend recently said that if an actress and a director in Hollywood have been married for thirty-four years, it should really be calculated in dog years.

What I discovered is that this particular guy never felt the need to control me. If anything, I've been the more controlling person. I have even at times, hypocritically, expected him to do the more "manly" chores, such as:

1. Taking out the garbage. (Sorry, I can't help it, I still think that's a guy's thing.)
2. Recording shows on our VCR. (Yeah, see, that's why I need his help.)
3. Basically any job that requires a tool. (Except for my vibrator. I'm fine with that one.)
4. Unplugging the toilets. (Just . . . please.)

He also tends to clean up after me more than I do after him. Still, I am always the one who goes downstairs at three in the morning brandishing the baseball bat to see why our three dogs are barking—but only because Tommy is sound asleep upstairs, confident in the knowledge that I am certifiably insane.

My husband, at times, still leaves his wet towel on our bed. And yeah, occasionally it makes me want to strangle him with it. But mostly, all I feel is a slight tug of irritation. After so long, it's dawned on me that he really, truly doesn't expect me to pick it up.

These days, I might throw it in the hamper. Or perhaps even leave it there. I guess I finally trust that sometimes a wet towel is . . . just a wet towel.

Not too bad. Only took me 238 years.

8

The Street Where "They" Lived

CHRISTMAS EVE, 1958. My family took our annual driving tour of all the extravagantly decorated houses in our suburban Michigan town. Twelve-foot-tall plastic Santas on rooftops, Nativity scenes with stuffed baby Jesuses gracing front lawns, trees and shrubs exploding with multicolored string lights; the neighborhood was lit up like a Christian shopping mall on steroids.

Then we suddenly found ourselves on a dark street that looked like a ghost town. While traditional colonial and redbrick houses lined the rest of our town, these homes were all made of concrete and glass. We drove through this foreign world as if we were on safari, peering out from the safety of our locked, faux-wood-trimmed Mercury station wagon.

"This is where the Jews live," whispered my father, as though he was the guide and didn't want to disturb the wildlife. "As you can see, these houses here are all very modern and *ostentatious*." It was the first time I remember hearing that word.

"Well, this is different," said my mom, noticing the houses' lack of holiday accessorizing.

"Holy mackeroly! Why don't they have any decorations?" I asked.

"They don't believe in Christmas." Dad spoke with a sense of wonder and pity, as if he were saying "They don't believe in food."

I instantly imagined these Jewish people wandering around their cheerless rooms like Scrooge in *A Christmas Carol*, dressed in drab clothes, murmuring "Bah, humbug" under their breath to each other. Even at eight years old, I was still enchanted by Christmas. I'd heard vicious rumors that Santa Claus was made up, but I wouldn't have any of it. I thought about how Santa must simply fly over these homes—"Skip this godforsaken street, Rudolph; Jews live here!" I pictured all the toy-deprived Jewish children and just didn't understand it. Why would anybody choose not to celebrate Christmas? And why were all of these nonbelievers living on only these few bleak blocks?

While growing up, as far as I could tell, I never met a Jew. There may have been some Jewish kids in the public schools I attended, but I wasn't aware of it. I was pretty sure Jewish people were not allowed at Red Run, the country club we belonged to, either. One day, after visiting an exclusively Jewish club for the first time with a friend who'd been invited, Dad came home and reported, "Oh, it was fine, except while I was taking a Jacuzzi, I looked down and there were human stools floating around. I jumped out of there fast!"

He said it as if he wasn't surprised, given that it was a Jewish club. Well, geez, I thought, if they shit in hot tubs, maybe I'm glad I don't know any Jews. He also absurdly implied that once the shit was spotted, nobody else bothered to get out. What was wrong with these people? I thought. Raccoons wouldn't have stayed in that hot tub!

My family spent summers on a lake in northern Michigan. I don't think there were many Jews there, either. The summer residents seemed more like the decorating, Christmas-celebrating type, our type. Everyone acted like they were always celebrating something. They looked ostentatiously cheery, wearing bright colors that matched their fruity cocktails. The yacht club we belonged to was exclusive, but it resembled a large rustic log cabin. Most of its members seemed to belong in an L.L.Bean catalog; men with nautical hats and madras Bermuda shorts, women in their capris and sun visors, sailboats with names like *Seas the Day*, *Aqua Holic*, and *Passing Wind*.

The bubble in which I grew up didn't just have a problem with Jews, by the way. My exposure to people of color was equally nonexistent—pretty much limited to Lorraine, our once-a-week cleaning lady, who had no last name that I ever heard, and the waiters at Red Run, one who I only heard my dad refer to as "Jimmy." Once in a while I'd see some Mexican gardeners tending our neighbors' lawns. The single most exotic place I'd ever visited before high school was Colorado.

Then I went to the University of Michigan and discovered diversity. It was like never leaving the flats of the Midwest your whole life and then suddenly driving up the coast of Big Sur. A Buddhist professor from India taught one of my favorite courses, Comparative Religion, where I learned about the Bible and the Koran. I had classmates and teachers from all over the globe. For the first time I was surrounded by Jews, Blacks, Muslims, and Hispanics from various economic backgrounds.

Attending a lot of Thank God It's Friday frat parties my freshman year, I gravitated to the one Jewish fraternity in particular. To my surprise, these guys looked exactly like everyone else and were not at all Scrooge-like. They even wore bright colors. A couple seemed especially fascinating— they had long, dark hair and were whip-smart, funny, and from the most sophisticated place on earth, New York City!

Although I entered that college as Republican as my parents, the conservative scales fell from my eyes faster than you could say "LSD." Then, after graduating, my new progressive values and I moved to New York; a city of millions, the most cosmopolitan, diverse place in the world. Yet for many years there I managed to have relationships only with WASPy men who looked and acted a lot like my father—cool, calm, and repressed.

Finally, at thirty-two, I ended up meeting and falling in love with a passionate Jew named Tommy Schlamme. One Christmas, I brought him home.

All eight of us sat around the red-cloth-covered table on Christmas Eve, wearing our red outfits. So many lit candles adorned our dining room, it resembled high mass in

Saint Patrick's Cathedral. Tommy sat next to me, wearing a long-sleeved black T-shirt.

"So, Tommy, tell us, how do your people celebrate Christmas?" my dad asked, his cheeks flushed from his extra-dry martini. I wanted to dive headfirst into my bowl.

Tommy swallowed a few thick spoonfuls of Mom's pea soup before answering. "Well, Dr. Lahti, exactly the same way your people celebrate Hanukkah," replied my future husband. We all laughed awkwardly. Then silence, interrupted only by the clanking of heavy silver spoons against china.

One of my brothers changed the subject. "How about those Wolverines?" he asked, referring to the U of M football team that my dad worshiped.

I looked over at Tommy and whispered, horrified, "How about these Lahtis?" It felt like I was watching my Christmas-sweater-clad family in a bad holiday episode of *Leave It to Beaver.*

Tommy must have thought he'd landed in an alternate universe. I'm pretty sure it was the first time he'd seen an entire family, all adults by this point, with outfits that matched their tablecloth. He also watched as Dad played the organ and we sang rapturous songs about the birth of Jesus Christ our Lord and Savior and Mommy kissing Santa Claus, often in well-rehearsed two- and three-part harmonies.

Born and raised in Texas, Tommy also didn't have a lot of experience with snow. I doubt it ever occurred to him that the thing to do with snow was to get naked and roll in it. Which is exactly what we all did after taking a sauna that night. With only towels wrapped around us, we ran out into the backyard in bare feet and lay down in the middle of enormous snow drifts. (The copious amounts of wine consumed at dinner helped, as did the cocktails before and the cognac after.)

At first Tommy, still in his black T-shirt, just observed the rest of us. With bare bodies steaming like freshly boiled shrimp, we pranced out into the frigid snow, yelling, "Woohoo! Come on, Tommy! It doesn't feel cold, it just tingles!" Then he watched as I lay down in six inches of the stuff and scissored my arms and legs up and down, creating a snow angel. "Come on," I encouraged him. "It's really good for you! Then we'll go back in the sauna and beat ourselves silly with birch branches!" Tommy finally joined in. But he appeared confused and skeptical, as if he'd just joined a family of inebriated polar bears.

The next day, some of my parents' friends stopped by. Penny Taylor, our next-door neighbor, met Tommy. She was also from Texas.

"So nAHce to meet you, Sammy."

"It's Tommy, Penny," I corrected her.

"Oh, sorry, AH knew that! So, are you EYE-talian?" she asked.

"No, I'm Jewish," Tommy chimed in.

"Oh, AH apologAHze! AH've just never seen black curly hair like yours, Sammy, and assumed you had to be—"

"How about those Wolverines, Penny?" I interrupted.

The second time I brought Tommy home, it was summer. We went to our family's cottage. The first thing he witnessed was my father's 6:00 a.m. assassination of a woodpecker with his 22-gauge shotgun. I doubt Tommy had ever seen a loaded firearm up close. The pest had pecked one too many holes on the side of our cottage, so Dad, in his red-plaid bathrobe, pulled his gun out of his drawer, aimed it up into the trees, fired once, and down floated a bird, as dead as an autumn leaf.

That afternoon my father took Tommy to the local golf course, which had probably never encountered a Jew, either.

As he placed his tee in the grass, Tommy remarked "Wow, this is great! We've practically got the course to ourselves!"

"Shhhhh, lower your voice! It disturbs the other players," Dad said, practicing his swing in his salmon polyester trousers.

Then that night, while we swam in the lake after another sauna, Dad came out on the dock and whispered, "Shhhh, Tommy, the neighbors! Your voice carries across the lake!" Yes, Tommy had a tendency to speak loudly, but I'd never heard my father shush any of his six booming-voiced children. Was it because he thought Jews not only defecated in hot tubs but were too boisterous on golf courses and large bodies of water?

Tommy wasn't a stranger to discrimination. His family had fled Nazi Germany while many of his relatives were exterminated in the concentration camps. Once, when he was growing up in Houston, a heavyset neighborhood woman sat him on her lap and hugged his six-year-old head into her ample bosom. "Poor child. You poor, poor child. I'm so sorry that you're going to go to Hell because you don't believe in Jesus," she cried, as she combed through his curly hair, looking for his horns. Tommy went home and asked his mom if that really was the case. "Couldn't we please, please, *please* just believe in Jesus? I mean, why not?" he begged.

I thought for sure that once he got to know Tommy, my father would realize just how uninformed he'd been. But instead I found out how pernicious unconscious prejudice can be. Many years after we married and had three young children, Tommy and Dad had an ongoing joke about which college football team was better—Ohio State or Michigan.

"Ohio is clearly superior, Ted. They're going to trounce your pathetic Wolverines!" teased Tommy, during a visit at my parents' place. He could have cared less about either team.

My dad laughed. "Ha, ha, ha, over my dead body!"

"You know what, Ted?" Tommy responded. "I so believe in my beloved Buckeyes that I'm willing to wager a whopping six dollars that they win."

Michigan won. Dad gloated and teased Tommy the rest of the night, all with warm humor.

For several years afterward Tommy would taunt my father back by saying "Oh, hmmm, I just don't seem to have that six bucks on me right now, but I know that Ohio will beat your crappy team this time." After about three years of this banter, Dad asked to speak with Tommy alone, down in the garage of our recently purchased home.

"Yeah, Tommy, you know you still owe me six dollars from that bet we made," declared Dad, sucking repeatedly on his pipe. "Maybe you don't think you have to honor that, but I just hope you aren't teaching my grandchildren that it's okay to welch on a bet."

My husband grabbed his wallet, yanked out six singles, said "Here's your money, Ted," and walked away. He came upstairs to our bedroom and paced back and forth, trying to process the staggering audacity of this mostly absentee father giving *him* parenting advice.

After this confrontation, Tommy and I both decided that we were just going to have to accept my dad's limitations. Though he loved Tommy, my father's coded anti-Semitism was part of his DNA, probably handed down from his parents, who in turn learned it from theirs. Admittedly, when Tommy and I first met, I jokingly referred to gefilte fish as mystery Jew-food and considered it a slippery slope to *payot* and those big black furry hats.

Neither Tommy nor I were at all religious as adults, but after becoming a couple we celebrated both Christmas and Hanukkah together, although to vastly different degrees. I remember one of our first Christmas Eves after we had kids. As soon as we all decorated our towering Frazier fir tree, which smelled like a pine forest, I rummaged through our stacks of boxes and found some sleigh bells.

With the Mormon Tabernacle Choir belting "O Holy Night" in the background, I said, "God, Tommy, remember when my dad asked you how 'your people' celebrated Christmas?" We both laughed. Sipping my eggnog, I then asked him if he wouldn't mind going up to the attic, shaking the bells, and stomping around so the children would believe Santa was on the roof. After they went to bed, as I placed the large quantity of meticulously wrapped presents under our tree, I pointed to the plate of freshly baked Christmas cookies. "Hey, Tommy, could you please take a few bites so the kids will think that Santa snacked on them?"

Tommy was a good sport and went along with all of it, and I loved watching as he seemed to get swept up in the silly magic of the holiday. But I couldn't help but notice that our home was smothered in wreaths, garlands, poinsettias, and twinkle lights. Carols played ad nauseam, flooding our home with the spirit of Christmas—while there was nary a trace of the spirit of the Hanukkah story.

As much as I'd fought against it, I was at times, unwittingly, still my father's daughter. As I hung all our vintage stockings on the fireplace mantel, I looked over and saw a lone menorah sitting like a dried-up, forgotten plant on a table in a dim corner of the family room—as dark and set apart as that street where "they" lived.

9

Mississippi Baby

'M THE ONLY actress in the history of show business who *lost* a part because she slept with the director. I was cast in my husband's film *Miss Firecracker*; but by the time they got around to shooting a year later, I was too pregnant to play the role. Rubbing salt into that oozing wound, I had to move, relatively last-minute, to Yazoo City, Mississippi, for two months to be with him for our baby's birth. So with my new seventy pounds of baby I relocated—in June—to the deepest bowels of the South. It's a debt to me that Tommy is still paying off.

Being eight months pregnant in the middle of summer in Yazoo City was like being eight months pregnant on the planet Mercury. Having never spent any time in the South, it felt like a wildly different planet. Tommy had to work sixteen-hour days. I knew no one there. A tsunami of homesickness hit me within the first few hours.

You could taste that particular kind of heat, not unlike tasting somebody's meal after it's been left outside in the sun for two weeks. The streets were eerily empty and quiet; there was no small talk from the mailmen. Even the neighborhood dogs just did their business and got the hell back inside. I rarely ventured out of our violently air-conditioned house my first week there. Even my short waddle down the sidewalk to our car left me dripping wet and ready for a nap.

One day our unborn baby and I had escaped into our usual sleep-stupor when Tommy came home from shooting and reminded me that our due date was in *six weeks*. Somehow, in the middle of this miserable hellhole, I needed to pull it together and find someone who would deliver our baby.

We both wanted a natural birth for a lot of reasons, mostly because the Lamaze classes we took in New York brainwashed us into thinking any pain medication would shrink our baby's brain to the size of a gnat. Besides, I loved the image of myself as the Earth Mother goddess that I saw in all my hippie birthing books, squatting in a field of golden wheat, backlit by the setting sun. It excited me that I might have that kind of pioneer-woman strength. More than all of that, though, I didn't want to be my mother. She'd been knocked out by general anesthesia for all *eight* of her C-sections—six babies and two stillborns. She was a vessel, sliced and diced, never a participant, never in control. I wanted control, no anesthesia, not even an epidural. Everyone knew epidurals were for sissies.

Luckily, right away we found a midwife in nearby Jackson who was a progressive feminist. But we still needed

to choose our doctor . . . and quickly. The first one we
met looked like he belonged on a box of Kentucky Fried
Chicken; chubby, with a short white beard and a rosy face
as if he'd just chugged a fifth of Jack Daniel's. He seemed a
little too impressed by my being a "celebrity."

"Well, Christine and Tommy, we're all so honored and
excited that you came all the way down to Mississippi to
have your baby! Especially since it has the highest infant
mortality rate in the country!" He leaned forward across
his messy desk and touched my hand. "But don't you worry,
sweetheart, you'll be just fine."

*Yes, I will be fine, as soon as I get the hell out of your
office!*

I'd wanted to come down here to support my husband,
but I had a brilliant obstetrician who I adored back in New
York City, and the doctors we met down here—all male—
validated every prejudice I had about the South. One of
them shook his head as we expressed our desire for a natural birth, glaring at us as if we might be part of some kind
of satanic cult. Finally we found one who agreed, but he
had a signed photo of himself with his arm around George
Wallace on the wall of his office. I just couldn't.

Time was running out; our baby could arrive any day
now. I started thinking I'd made a huge mistake ever leaving New York. Then we met Dr. Beverly McMillan. A female
doctor in Mississippi? Had the heat caused me to halluci-
nate her? She had a delicate-looking face with no-nonsense
short-cropped brown hair. Her Victorian house, perched on
a green hill overlooking Jackson, was decorated with faded
Persian rugs and antique furniture. She served us tea in

vintage floral china cups with perfectly unmatched vintage saucers. We sat in her wood-paneled library with its Tiffany lamps and its floor-to-ceiling bookshelves. I watched her closely as she sipped her tea; her little finger charmingly stuck straight out.

We made our pitch and then eagerly awaited her response. She put down her cup and, in a warm southern drawl, said, "I am so impressed that y'all want to do this naturally. I've been trying to encourage my patients to do it this way for years, but they are very resistant. It's like the women's movement hasn't made it this far south yet."

Practically crying with relief, Tommy and I smiled at each other; we had found our gal! After we said our goodbyes, we almost skipped down her crunchy gravel driveway, which was where we saw the bumper stickers plastered all over a red pickup truck parked there.

ABORTION IS MURDER

PRO-LIFE SAVES LIVES

ABORTION IS THE ULTIMATE CHILD ABUSE

GUNS DON'T KILL PEOPLE, ABORTION CLINICS DO

I'd been a prochoice activist my entire adult life. Tommy shared my view that protecting women's reproductive freedom was of dire importance. So we stood in silence for a few seconds before heading straight for our car.

"I think a storm is coming in," said my husband as he pulled onto the road.

"That would be nice. Might cool things off a bit," I muttered, my arms tightly folded on my whale lap.

We drove for about a minute. Then Tommy said, "Look, I know we don't have any more time, but maybe we should think about looking for another doctor . . ."

"No, I know. I agree. I mean, we *have* to. Absolutely," I said, stepping on his words.

"Or maybe you should think about going back to New York," he said sadly.

"But I really want us to be together for this! Besides, I'm not sure any airline will let me fly this late in the game." I looked down at my near-bursting belly. A foot the size of my thumbnail kicked me hard. I saw it bulging through my tight T-shirt. I gasped. He looked over at me. I looked at him. By the time we got home, we decided that the truck couldn't possibly belong to Dr. McMillan. She was a sophisticated, liberal, pro-woman doctor with great taste in interior decorating!

So, our doctor chosen, I spent the next few weeks hanging out on Tommy's set. It was 103 degrees, 100 percent humidity. My enlarged inner thighs made loud sweat-slap sounds with every step I took. Scared to move because I might ruin a take, I sat there, trapped, wondering how many other parts I'd have to turn down because I had a child. Tommy promised me I wouldn't have to give up my career, but what did he know? He was a man. He wasn't the one who had to watch another actor play the hell out of *his* part. He didn't have to munch on roll after roll of fruit-flavored extra-strength Tums to try to ease *his* chronic heartburn; he wasn't the one worried he might distract the actors with the sound of *his* wet flabby thighs.

A few days later, I woke up from a nightmare. I dreamed

that I didn't have a baby inside me but rather a little yellow duck—an actual fluffy baby duck. Upset, I jumped out of bed, and suddenly my water broke, a week early.

Tommy and I rushed to the hospital in Jackson. We were taken to our private "birthing room." I had envisioned something spa-like; softly lit, painted in warm neutrals, with antique furniture and an appropriately faded Persian rug. But this one had insulting ceiling lights and was decorated like a girlie-girl's fantasy bedroom; all pinks and yellows, with painted flowers, kittens, and yes, baby ducks smothering the walls.

For the first few hours I thought, Hey, come on, this labor stuff isn't so bad. Are all these southern women just a bunch of wusses? What are they so afraid of? Maybe they don't have decent Lamaze classes down here. Perhaps they didn't learn, like I did, that pain could be mastered simply by being in charge!

Then, by about the tenth hour, things started to get real. Sadly, that breathing technique we'd practiced for months turned out to be a heinous lie, like being told to just take an aspirin after being hit by a train.

"Owwww! It feels like he's punching his way out of my lower back!" I yelled. Our strong midwife rubbed my back then handed me a tennis ball. "Here, Christine. This should help. Just gently roll back and forth over it." I knew she meant well, but in that moment, all I wanted to do was take that ball and gently shove it up her ass.

Nurses' heads kept popping into our doorway. All their southern accents sounded exactly the same, like they were in an episode of *The Andy Griffith Show.*

"Oh, honey, are you ok*aye*? Can *Ah* offer you something to make you more comfortable?"

"No! I'm not doing any of that! I told you guys!" I screamed. "I'm fff . . . *ahhh* . . . ine!"

"Ok*aye*," she replied, sighing deeply, as if I'd said I was jumping out of a plane without a parachute.

About an hour later, another nurse came in. "Excuse me, sir. What is going on? We are all very concerned. It sounds like someone's *dah*-in' in here!" She had to yell to be heard because by this point I was screaming bloody murder. "Look, *Ah*'m terribly sorry, but some of the other women are complainin'. Do you think you could get her to take something?"

Jesus Christ. This was a women's hospital. Yet all they wanted to do was shut us up. I proceeded to bellow so loud, I was sure I scared the other newborns on my floor back up the vaginas of their sedated mothers.

After twenty hours of trying to push a house past my cervix, my teeth chattering, my entire body started to go into convulsions. Beginning to panic, I breathlessly asked my husband, "Remind me again why we decided to do this naturally?!" Just then the doors opened and in walked Dr. McMillan, who had been in and out all day, checking on my progress. I immediately begged her to give me some drugs—"Just something mild that won't make the baby's brain shrivel up!" She gently took my hand and offered me a sedative called Stadol.

"This should just take the edge off a bit," she reassured me.

"YES, PLEASE! NOW!" I cried. I knew I was letting

everyone down; our son, our midwife, the Lamaze train-
ers, my husband, and myself, not to mention the entire
women's movement, but I didn't give a shit. Within seconds it put me to sleep, only to be woken up by a magnitude 9 earthquake in my uterus every few minutes. Loopy
and completely out of control now, I felt at the mercy of
Dr. McMillan.

After working painstakingly to get the baby into a
proper position, she at long last asked me to push, three
times. But by this point, I wasn't focused on pushing out a
baby; I was just trying with all my might to push out the
pain.

Finally, after twenty-two hours of labor, our son arrived.
As he lay peacefully on my stomach, both of us beyond
exhaustion, I looked down and saw that he was perfect;
the opposite of a duck. Standing around me I noticed our
heroic and patient doctor, our hardworking midwife, the
worried nurses, and my husband, who had tears rolling
down his cheeks.

I felt such gratitude toward the entire staff. That is,
until they started making fun of our baby's first name,
which we had chosen carefully so he wouldn't be teased
like young Tommmmeeee Schlammmmmeeee had been.

In fact, we'd spent months trying to figure out what he
was going to be called. It had seemed completely absurd
to me that our child would automatically be given his father's last name. Of course, we had the hyphenated option,
but both Lahti-Schlamme and Schlamme-Lahti sounded
dreadful, as did the combo "Schlahti."

I'd said, "You know, honey, I think we can both agree

that Lahti is a prettier *sounding* name." Slam dunk, I thought.

Then my husband reminded me, "Well, that may be true, sweetie, but as you know, most of my relatives were . . . uh . . . exterminated in the concentration camps, so . . . um . . . you know . . . there are very few Schlammes left." He played *the Holocaust card.* Those fucking Jews!

But in spite of all that agonizing over his name, within the very first hour of our son's Mississippi birth, we heard, "Wilson Hugo Laydee Schlam? Why don't this baby have a first name? Which one is his last name?" It was asked by a stocky, thick-necked nurse as she read his chart. We could hear her chortling all the way down the hall. I hugged my baby close to my chest. It was time to pack our bags and get the hell out of Mississippi.

Several years later, Tommy and I were back in our beloved Upper West Side apartment in New York. While reading the Sunday *Times*, we noticed an article about a man named Roy McMillan from Jackson who was a self-proclaimed "abortion abolitionist." He was quoted as saying, "It is not a sin to kill abortionists." He would harass the patients at the local clinic by yelling in a child's voice, "Please don't kill me, Mommy! Keep me away from all those bloody hands!" He'd then throw little plastic naked babies into their car windows, or if that didn't work, he'd show them Ziploc bags of severed fetus parts.

"McMillan, McMillan," I said, "that sounds familiar." We turned the page and saw a picture of him with our beloved ob-gyn. "Oh my God, that's Dr. Bev McMillan! Holy shit! That *was* her fucking truck!" Apparently, after opening the first abortion clinic in Mississippi, she saw the born-again Christian light and joined her husband's radical mission. In that moment I was horror-stricken; the first hands that touched my baby were the hands of a right-wing nutcase who believed sperm were squiggly children!

"Oh, those motherfucking self-righteous assholes! How dare she not tell us this before we agreed to—" I started to rant.

Then I heard our toddler playing across the room. I watched him toss each of his favorite Beanie Babies, sending them soaring into the air, then erupting with giggles as stuffed unicorns, bears, and giraffes rained down onto his tiny body.

In that instant, I knew that if I ran into Dr. McMillan on the street, I would have to hug her. When we needed her, we were certainly able to put aside the fact that she was rabidly antichoice. After all, it was her capable, life-giving hands that brought our son into the world.

Wilson Hugo Lahti Schlamme, I am proud to say, has grown up to be a gifted artist, and a prochoice feminist. Late at night, there are times I can't help but wonder if his occasional, unfortunate tendency to watch Fox News has something to do with where he was born. But as I picture our remarkable, tender son, there's no question that my husband's debt to me was paid off a long time ago. And then some.

10

Losing Virginity

We vow to stay virgins until marriage," my best
friend Pam and I whisper-swore to each other,
linking our freshly manicured pinkies together. Now se-
niors in high school, we'd already bonded as blood sisters
in third grade. We'd pricked our fingers with my mom's
sewing needle, and then kissed the drops of blood together.
Today we confirmed our virginity sisterhood.

We weren't about to follow in "stacked Wendy's" X-rated
footsteps. Although none of us had any actual proof that
she went "all the way," we'd shunned her since junior
high. She sure as hell looked like she did, with those pointy
boobs that strained the pearl buttons on her tight cardi-
gans, that bottle-blond hair. She didn't have many friends,
except for all the boys who waddled after her like little
ducklings. She sashayed around the cafeteria, much too
comfortable in that busty body of hers. The slut.

Pam and I were adamant about heading off to college with our respect and hymens intact, goddamn it. Besides, I'd already learned from my dad that having sex without being "in love" and married would be the biggest mistake I could ever make, as dire as drinking a gallon of cyanide. His favorite mantra—"Why buy the cow if you can get the milk for free?"—made complete sense to me at the time. Nobody was taking *my* only valuable commodity without putting a fucking ring on it!

So I waited and waited and waited some more for "love" to arrive. But it never did. Who knew what love even meant? When you couldn't live without someone? If your heart stopped when you saw him enter a room? When you got misty holding his hand? If you simply had to have a baby with him? Centuries away from having any of those feelings, I assumed I'd have to stay a virgin for the rest of my life.

Throughout the remainder of high school and well into my sophomore year in college, I remained true to our pact. Somehow, blow jobs and getting fondled and fingered were permissible with just a "like" or "almost love," but penis-in-vagina penetration still had to be saved for the whole "true love" shebang.

Then, at nineteen, I started feeling like the oldest living virgin at the University of Michigan. After all, this was the pre-AIDS era of free love! After quitting the sorority that proudly claimed to have the most coeds engaged to be married, I evolved into an antimarriage, pro-making-love-not-war activist. Except I hadn't made any love. After shamefully confessing my inexperience to my flower-child

friends, I'd hear "You're a freak, Chris! What are you waiting for? Just get it the fuck over with!" What *was* I holding out for, and why? Because of my *dad*? That seemed
messed up in so many ways. So after several boyfriends
came close, literally millimeters close, I finally decided I
would lose this albatross once and for all.

I woke up that Indian-summer Saturday morning in
1969 knowing this would be the day. I got semi-dolled-up
in my best clothes—tie-dyed bell-bottoms with a tank
top—and headed to the Diag, the meadowlike place on
campus where I'd spent many an afternoon sitting on the
grass, harmonizing Crosby, Stills & Nash's "Helplessly
Hoping" and Joni Mitchell's "Free Man in Paris" with
friends. I perched myself on a bench and let the games
begin.

Contrary to all my brainwashing, I set out to have my
first full sexual encounter with a complete stranger. Of
course, I had no idea if anyone would be interested, but I
felt confident I'd eventually find a willing party. I sat there
silently rating every boy who strolled past. I didn't know
exactly what I was searching for. Probably someone tall
and handsome, definitely freshly showered. Most importantly, I couldn't know the guy or give a shit about him.

I watched the unsuspecting parade of potential lovers
go by for about an hour. Then I saw him: a lanky, sandy-
haired boy sitting across from me. As he read his high-
lighted copy of Alan Watts's *Wisdom of Insecurity*, I prayed
he would soon be mine. He looked model gorgeous, kind,
possibly even a little shy. I approached my target and asked
if I could join him. After chatting for a while about our

mutually beloved book and the unseasonable weather, we decided to go to a nearby coffee shop.

First, I inquired about his family and his major, but I didn't listen to his answers. I lit a cigarette. Then took a deep inhale.

"So I know this is going to sound weird and more than a little abrupt, but I'm very attracted to you, and I'm really sick of being a virgin. So . . . is there any way you might want to go to your apartment and fuck?" I took another puff, trying to look cooler and more casual than I felt. I had two nosey roommates at the time who I knew would be home, so my place wasn't an option.

"Uhhhh, really? Okay, um, sure," said the man, whose name I don't remember, laughing.

Most women I knew rarely screwed on the first date. Even my counterculture girlfriends played the bases, consecutively. But you had to run the whole field first. So my virginity savior looked flabbergasted and a little like he'd just won the World Series.

Once at his tiny studio apartment, we smoked a joint. It suddenly got crickets-quiet except for the Moody Blues, the eight-track he'd popped into his player as soon as we'd arrived. Neither of us knew how to make the first move. So to break the ice, I asked, "Would you mind if we take off our clothes and do the mirror exercise first?" I'm not sure why I believed engaging in some naked sensitivity training together would enhance our encounter, but thankfully he agreed.

I'd recently learned "mirroring" in my acting class. Standing in front of your partner, you'd take turns leading a slow-motion movement while the other followed as precisely as possible. It supposedly built trust. So even if we weren't "in love," we could at least have a little spiritual bonding! Stoned, we mirrored each other to "Nights in White Satin," as if we were students in a nudist Twyla Tharp modern dance class. Then we laid down on his extra-long single bed.

High as kites, we could barely look at each other. Then I began to stare at this unknown person, hoping to will a connection with him. His eyes seemed cloudy and distant, like he might actually be thinking of his former girlfriend. However, something profoundly life-changing was about to occur (at least for me), and I sure as hell wasn't going to miss a second of it. Even if I had to fake it, even if I had to play both parts, I would make this as meaningful a movie in my head as possible.

It was over in a minute and a half. He came. I didn't. He gently stroked my cheek. I cried—but not because of any newly found intimacy. I just felt relieved not to be a virgin anymore. The whole affair proved hugely disappointing. Just like that time when, at eight years old, I devoured what looked like a large piece of homemade fudge off our kitchen counter, and it turned out to be a large piece of canned dog food.

Really? That's all? I thought as I lay lost in the shiny hairlessness of his chest. Jesus Christ. *That's* what I should never "lose"? Precisely what the fuck *was* I losing? And would I ever find it again?

I had to get to my Comparative Religion class. I didn't know what to say to him. "Thanks for the dick?" No, I thought, better to lie through my teeth. "Wow. Thanks for making this so special. I'll see you around sometime. Definitely!" I whispered, squeezing a hand that was softer than mine, peering one last time at his finely featured Adonis face.

I grew angry as I walked to class. Newly a feminist, I thought about how much I'd been duped. How rooted in misogyny was my (and my dad's) obsession with my precious virginity? My dad had never encouraged my brothers to save theirs for their future wives. Boys I knew who had lots of sex were considered studs. Girls who did got called whores. Having bought the whole women-as-property package for nineteen years, I wanted a full refund.

I wished my parents had told me that sex was beautiful and fun, especially with someone you care about. Instead of saving my virginity, why couldn't they have said . . . save your heart, or your talent, or your intelligence, for someone worthy of you? But they made my "cherry" the thing to guard, the most priceless gift I could give to someone.

I missed out on a lot of good sex in my early college years, but by the time I graduated and moved to New York City I had made up for lost time. In addition, my best girl-friend introduced me to the vibrator, which led to the discovery of whole new worlds within my body. Yes, it felt better to make love with men I knew and liked, but sometimes a one-nighter or all-by-myself sufficed just fine. At last I felt in charge. Well, almost in charge.

During this awakening, as a second-wave feminist, I also demanded to be valued for other things besides my body. So I devoted a lot of energy to obsessively downplaying, even denying, any potential sexiness. Of course, the effort to look not sexy took just as much time as it did to look sexy. I still tried hard to look like I didn't try.

A longtime boyfriend used to beg me to dress more "womanly." We literally wrote our lists of grievances and gave them to each other. I wanted him to be less threatened by my success and not chew with his mouth open. He wanted me to wear more makeup and dresses. I refused. Objectify myself?! Our culture did that all on its own without my help, thank you very much.

I'll never forget when a famous film director gave me some of his career advice. We were sitting next to each other on a dais at some awards event. "You're too busy looking for respect, Christine. You need to dirty yourself up and be more sexy," he said, as if "respect" and "sexy" were mutually exclusive.

It even took me a while to feel comfortable playing a very sexualized character like Maggie the Cat in *Cat on a Hot Tin Roof.* But I finally got inside her skin and understood her power (or lack thereof). She used her attractiveness to get what she wanted, but tragically it was the only value she felt she had.

As recently as a few years ago, I found myself confused about Kim Kardashian. I mean, wait just a feminist fuckin' minute! Selling herself as a sex object and calling it "empowering"? Isn't that like eating ketchup and calling it a vegetable? I regarded her as kind of a joke, an extremely rich joke, with a massive social media following: an insecure narcissist desperate for attention.

Then I learned from third-wave feminists that, just like

when we bullied Wendy in high school, I was "slut sham-
ing" Kim Kardashian; that she actually had full control
of her "art" and was merely celebrating her beauty and
sexuality. Who was I to grade her feminism? God knows
I'd flunked mine on numerous occasions. Hello, Joy dishwashing liquid!

These millennials have taught me that their "pro-sex
feminism" is the undeniable next step in empowerment.
If men choose to regard them as "objects," tough shit,
that is their problem. Men aren't exploiting them; these
women call their own shots, fully in charge and embold-
ened. Unlike myself and many of my generation, maybe
these bright, brazen young women grew up already com-
prehending their full worth. They didn't have to prove,
downplay, or hide anything.

Evolving as a feminist has been as messy and complicated for me as it has been essential. It's not been easy to
keep up sometimes. I've had to reckon with my own sexism
when I've also judged women for other choices—like being
stay-at-home moms. (Wasn't the whole point simply that
they had a choice?)

My generation thought we had all the answers. Clearly
we didn't. These younger women will find more of them.
Hopefully, a part of their evolution will include challenging this absurd concept of virginity that we were shackled
with.

I recently heard about brides in China who surgically
restore their hymens so that their husbands can believe
they are still virgins. And hundreds of young women are
actually selling their virginities online. It's a big thing, ap-

parently. Why can't we females just own our sexuality as simply one of the many powerful things about ourselves? Instead of obsessing about saving it, selling it, or losing it, perhaps we should just lose the whole notion of it altogether. Why can't losing our virginity be just another glorious rite of passage, like taking our first road trip or voting for the first time or tasting our first glass of a Tuscan Barolo?

If you're reading this and you're one of the boys I left confused and frustrated back then, I'd like to say I'm sorry—I was confused and frustrated, too. But more importantly, I'd like to apologize to Wendy. You didn't deserve our gossip. You just scared us. You were onto something. Positively, beautifully, ahead of your time.

11

Kidnapped

N 1986 THE ticking of my biological time clock became deafening. While my husband had been eager to start a family for several years, I still felt ambivalent, reluctant to stop working even for a minute. I'd always just assumed I'd be one of those older actresses wearing the T-shirt with the picture of a woman holding her aghast face saying, "Oops! I can't believe I forgot to have children!"

Besides, I couldn't quite locate my "maternal instinct." It was just nowhere to be found. I didn't even feel the urge when I'd meet friends' babies. They all looked like mini Winston Churchills, and I'd always have to fake the gushing. And it wasn't clear to me exactly what I should be searching for when it came to that instinct. Girlfriends described their desire for having a child as an "undeniable, gnawing *hunger* to have a child, like you can't feel whole unless you have one." I only *hungered* like that for an Oscar, an African safari, and hot-fudge sundaes with walnuts. Even though it seemed I was born without that mothering urge, I didn't feel too concerned about it; it was just like missing a toenail or the ability to do a backbend.

But finally, after doing the movie *Housekeeping*, something creatively profound was satisfied in me. At last I felt sufficiently established in my career. So I figured it might be a good time to start thinking about starting a family. Besides, it wasn't that I didn't want to be a mom, I just didn't want to be *my* mom. And the only way to prevent that was to make sure certain mandatory conditions were understood and accepted.

"Okay, fine, I'm ready to have kids now, but we need to be perfectly clear about the rules," I announced to my husband, referencing a key chapter from one of my dog-eared feminist handbooks. "We have to be completely equal partners, Tommy, all responsibilities shared fifty/fifty. We're both going to be breadwinners, why shouldn't we both be hands-on raising our children? Just because I'll be the mother, don't go assuming that I'm automatically the 'primary' parent."

Tommy agreed without hesitation. I wasn't surprised. From the moment I met him, I knew he'd be an all-in father. In fact, it was one of the reasons I'd married him. As I prepared to throw away my diaphragm, I decided I'd just have to time the pregnancy somehow to occur during the slower months of movie and TV casting.

But I never got the memo that by the time you're thirty-seven, your eggs, just like your breasts, won't be quite as sprightly as they once were. It had never occurred to me that I should have frozen a few of those suckers back in my early thirties. Month after month, our high hopes were crushed by those few drops of blood in my underwear. After seeing an infertility specialist and requiring many hormone injections, I was starting to feel like I'd never wanted anything more in my life.

But wait, was this partly because I couldn't do it? Could this be similar to one of those acting parts I became obsessed about getting because I was told I was "too tall"? Or were those fucking hormones responsible, the ones that forced my ovaries to churn out eight eggs per month instead of the one wrinkly, gasping, thirty-seven-year-old egg? I didn't have a clue. Until I got pregnant.

Those first two months were surprisingly sublime. I thought maybe what grew inside me was not only a human life but also a real maternal proclivity. We knew enough not to tell too many people, so I secretly started imagining a life with a family in it. Everything I looked at, I saw through the lens of our future child—things like a shoe box, a spiderweb, and mud all seemed remarkable and newly invented. Objects took on a kind of sheen I'd never before imagined—except during that one good acid trip in college when I beheld a pinecone for two hours as if, within its scaly brown body, it held all seven of the wonders of the world.

Then, at exactly ten weeks into my pregnancy, I took a long bike ride in the Hamptons with my husband. That night I started to bleed. My doctor said to take it easy, just get some bed rest. But when I got up in the middle of the night to pee, whatever was trying to be a baby fell out of me and splashed into the toilet bowl. I looked for signs of a person, the beginning of a head, maybe an arm bud or a leg sprout, but there was nothing but a gooey mass of black blood. "Not viable," my doctor told me. "Nothing to do with the bike ride. And no, your early ambivalence about having children didn't jinx it at all."

"Just not meant to be," friends said, trying to be supportive. I wanted to snap their necks. Didn't they know that I'd already heard his laugh and knew that he loved the wind as much as I did? Didn't they realize I'd made big plans for this person, that I already knew this child's favorite books would be *Goodnight Moon* and *Runaway Bunny*? That I'd even designed the silver-starred cardboard crowns he'd wear for his birthdays—like the ones my mom had made for me?

"Don't worry. There will be other children," one well-meaning friend said to me. That's like someone saying after your husband dies suddenly in a horrible car crash, "Don't worry, there will be other husbands."

It surprised me that the loss of this maybe-baby had left me so gutted. But after a few months of mourning and healing, we were ready to try again. Several more egg-boosting injections later, it took. Finally, viably pregnant! The first few nauseating months dragged by, but during months three through five, I felt creatively on fire. Not only was this life growing within me, but I got to bring to life one of my favorite characters, Alma in *Summer and Smoke*. I did worry what our developing fetus might be experiencing as I rode my character's emotional roller coaster every night, eight full-blown nervous breakdowns a week. As soon as I'd arrive home from the theater, I'd rush to play Mozart with the speakers lying on my belly to help calm any potential baby trauma.

Throughout my pregnancy, I also carefully repeated our parenting mantra to my husband: "Fifty/fifty, Tommyyyy, rememberrrrr, fiftyyyy/fiftyyyyyyyyy." I said it after I had to drop out of that play because I was no longer credible as a virginal spinster. I chanted it in our car on the way to our coed baby shower, and especially during my twenty-two hour, virtually pain-medication-free labor. "Puff, puff, pant pant, ARGH, puff puff, pant pant, DON'T FORGET, FIFTY MOTHERFUCKING FIFTY!!"

BUT RIGHT AFTER our baby Wilson was born, my concerns didn't center around Tommy's reneging. I feared I was going to be the worst mother on the planet. Even though I'd felt deeply connected with Wilson in utero, in reality I didn't have that instantaneous bond I expected. I got how daunting the responsibility was; this tiny human's life was literally in my hands. But I mostly just felt anxious to lose the seventy pounds I'd gained and get back to work. Jesus Christ, new mothers shouldn't feel that way, right?

Apparently fathers got a cultural pass. You always heard men say, "Nah, I didn't start to feel a connection to our baby until he was out of diapers." Or "Nope, didn't really feel close until they were old enough to play sports with me." And nobody batted an eye. The phrase "paternal instinct" didn't even exist in the English language! But moms had to be gobsmacked right out of the gate.

For the first few weeks, I kept having nightmares that

I'd forget about Wilson, accidentally leaving him in the car if I went to a café or to my spin class. Also, it was pretty uneventful—I mean, all he did was sleep, eat, fart, shit, sleep, eat, fart, and then . . . um . . . oh yeah, shit. Even though others swore he grinned—*Look! There it is! See? He's smiling! Awwww! That's definitely a smile!*—I always knew it was just gas. Because that's what my face often looked like when I farted.

Stuck at home alone, I became frantic that show business at large had forgotten all about me. My agents would soon stop returning my calls, casting people would start asking them for a Christine Lahti "type." *If* I ever worked again, I'd only get to play the "mom" parts, which were not only brain-paralyzingly boring, but always number fourteen on the call sheet. In spite of all my careful strategizing about how I would "have it all," it became clear that would only be possible if, like my character on *Chicago Hope* said, "I gave up eating, sleeping, and bathing."

In those early days, while Wilson lay next to me in bed, I feared I'd roll on top of him and squash him into a newborn pancake. I'd lie awake staring at him, in awe of the miracle that was his cheek, the poetry of his pillow lips. I watched as his doll hands instinctively knew to grasp my finger and hold on for dear life, the way a robin clings to its branch. If he cried, the comfort that my breast gave him seemed overwhelmingly powerful. Trying to match his breathing as it slowed and sped up again, I wanted to know what he dreamed . . . if he dreamed. I'd finally fall asleep, only to wake up next to a tiny stranger.

While nursing him in those early weeks, I'd try to make

eye contact with him. It was like trying to connect with a squirrel. Days passed as I searched for him. I wished I could somehow reach inside and pull him out. But Wilson would only hold my gaze for a few seconds, curious but mostly disinterested. Instead he'd make those rubbery, goofy grimaces, reminiscent of a pug's. And just like when seeing a pug's face, I'd laugh out loud but would always be somewhat alarmed.

Then, after about six weeks, we were sitting on his blue-gray rocking chair one late afternoon, the one that rolled more than rocked, like riding ocean waves. I had just finished feeding him and tried peering into his eyes as usual. He started to cry, and I saw he had a full diaper. I took him to his changing table to clean him up, and as he lay there, like he'd been underwater the whole time, the person who was my son surfaced, looked into my eyes, and smiled . . . through me.

Or maybe I'd been the one underwater this whole time. Perhaps I'd forgotten that loving someone and feeling connected to them takes a lot of hard work; that the more you put in, the more you get out.

My breath caught in my throat. My eyes filled with tears. I'd never felt so close to anyone in my life. Suddenly, as if I'd known him forever, I understood volumes about him. My heart exploded in ways I never knew possible, and I was a goner.

However, still committed to breaking all conventional rules, I felt determined to follow through on our parenting pact. Tommy, true to his word, shared all the responsibilities. He got as blissfully involved and connected as I was. We took turns doing everything: bathing, changing diapers, dressing, playing, rocking, snuggling, strolling, and burping. He'd even get up most nights for the dreaded 4:00 a.m. feeding. When one of us worked long hours, the other would simply pick up the slack. We spent two years all together in New York City, where our experiment in parity seemed a revolutionary, resounding success.

Then, between shows of *The Heidi Chronicles* on a late Saturday afternoon, this happened.

"YOU STOLE MY BABY! WHY DID YOU TAKE HIM FROM ME? WHY? WHYYYYY?" I screamed on the phone to my husband, sounding a lot like Nancy Kerrigan right after Tonya Harding had her knees whacked. Tommy had taken Wilson on a two-week trip to Los Angeles. I was in my musty dressing room at the Bernie Jacobs Theatre in NYC, surrounded by pictures of our now two-year-old son Scotch-taped to the mirrors.

"Wait . . . what?" Tommy asked, incredulously. "You've repeatedly said that we needed to—"

"I know what I said. But I can't stand this! Bring him back now! How dare you take him from me?" I sobbed.

I'd been supportive of this trip; in fact, I'd encouraged it. By this point, I hadn't been separated from Willie for more than a few hours at a time. But after doing eight grueling shows a week for several months, I thought this would be an opportunity to *really* put our arrangement to practice. Tommy would take Wilson with him to LA and be his primary parent for a while, while I got to focus on my work and catch up on much-needed rest. But after only a few hours, before they'd even arrived in California,

I found that my husband, in taking my baby away from me, had severed one of my arms.

Tommy called as soon as the plane landed. I begged him to bring Wilson back as soon as possible. At once our future became crystal clear. Not only would I have to take Wilson on location with me wherever I might be working, Tommy could never take him anywhere without me, except for an overnight camping trip. Maybe. I felt doubtful, in that moment, that I would ever be capable of separating from him. Even if he got married someday, I'd have to stay in a little bedroom decorated in tea-stained floral prints and vanilla-scented candles in the basement of his house.

Still heaving, I went on, "Okay, I know I've been insistent about this, but I'm going to need to amend our deal. I'm going to *have* to be the primary parent. It might actually have to be fifty-five/forty-five, or maybe even sometimes sixty/forty or sixty-one/thirty-nine, depending on the particular circumstances."

Tommy paused briefly before taking a deep breath. He then reassured me that he would indeed add that rider to our contract.

I hung up, then looked at my soaked eyes in the mirrors and wondered, as my husband surely did, if perhaps I had lost my mind. This wasn't supposed to happen! When the fuck had my son become one of my organs? When had his every disappointment, his every struggle, his every joy, become mine? I sank down into my creaky chair and focused on a picture of Wilson. It was a recent Polaroid of him taken at Serendipity's in New York City, spoon in hand, about to dive into a hot-fudge sundae (with walnuts) that was bigger than his head. His dimples looked like craters in his flushed round cheeks, and I couldn't tell where he ended and I began.

Tommy didn't kidnap my son by taking him to LA. Not by a long shot. I was the one who'd already been captured and held hostage, by a stealthy, blue-eyed, towheaded baby. One day when life interrupted my plans.

12

What I Wish I'd Known About Love Scenes

WISH THERE'D BEEN a class for actors called How to Do a Love Scene. They're not easy. They can be awkward and artificial, but somehow you need to make them seem relaxed and real. And you have to do them in front of several cameras, bright lights, and with a whole lot of strangers pretending not to watch. I had to learn the hard way.

Once you are on set and it's already too late, you start asking yourself all kinds of questions: How much do I really go for it? Should I discuss boundaries? What body parts, if any, are off-limits? While working, I've let guys know they could grope breasts and butt, but I've never been allowed to touch an actor's dick. My sex scenes have always been pretty tame; mostly just the foreplay or aftermath, with fake heavy breathing and several strategically placed sheets.

Over the years, I'm sure there've been complaints about

my uptight making-out skills. In the early days, I imagined my costars comparing notes. "Yuck! I've had better
kisses from my basset hound!" "Yeah, kissing her was like
smooching an elbow." Especially if I felt nervous, which
was true 99.9 percent of the time. Unless I'd had a glass of
chardonnay before. Which was also true 99.9 percent of
the time.

I've worked with several actors who also had no clue.
The most egregious "stage kiss" for me was early in my
career on Broadway, when a guy insisted on cramming
his massive tongue down my throat, no matter how hard
I tried to block it. This tongue felt like a slab of raw beef
that could feed a family of six.

I wanted to politely suggest a simple closed-mouth kiss.
But I knew this guy had a fragile ego. So I practiced how
the conversation *might* go . . .

"Ahh . . . Norman, can we talk about this kiss we have
to do in act two?"

"What do you mean, *have* to do?" I pictured his thick
unibrow rising to the top of his forehead.

"Ha ha! I mean, *get* to do. . . . It's just . . . could you,
uh . . . do ya think we could maybe keep our mouths
closed?"

"Wow, really? I'm getting notes on my kissing? Are you
saying I'm not good at it?" He'd most likely spit a little as
he said this, and I'd have to take a few steps back, making
it look like I was just shifting my weight.

"No, you're awesome! It's just . . . well . . . do you think
you could maybe not put your tongue in my mouth?"

"What? Jeez, I'm just like in the moment and we're

supposed to be playing two people who really dig each other, right?"

"No, I know. . . . It's just your tongue goes like really deep in. I mean, maybe it's because my mouth is so small or something, but . . ."

"Are you grossed out by my tongue, is that it?" he'd ask, his brow now in a furrowed, furry knot.

"No! Stop! You have an incredible tongue, it's one of the greatest tongues I've ever worked with. It's just . . . ugh, excuse me . . ." And then I would have to go throw up.

Once I tried pursing my lips so tightly, they looked like the anus on a Chihuahua. But without fail, Norman burrowed through. I nearly gagged. But I needed to somehow stay in character, remember my lines, and keep acting instead. As the run went on, he felt completely entitled to explore all the caverns of my mouth with his "mouth penis." (That's exactly what it was like. He should have been put into actor's prison for Statutory Mouth Rape by a Tongue!)

But the real problem lay with me. I never had that imagined conversation with my mouth assaulter. Because even though I had mighty feminist strength in my head, apparently my voice wasn't quite up to the task. At twenty-seven, a proverbial late bloomer, I remained unable to completely shed the thin skin of a second-class citizen.

Of course, now, if anything like that ever happened, I'd have had no problem asking him to kindly keep his tongue to himself. If he didn't, I might be inclined to bite it off and spit the slimy fucker down his throat.

I went on to have some great professional kisses, kisses

with respect and restraint. If any actress tells you that she hates those kind of love scenes, she's lying. "They're so hard!" she might whine. What is so hard about it? Please! What other profession pays you to cheat on your husband all in a day's work? I worked with some well-mannered, hot men on *Chicago Hope* and got to make out with several of them: Peter Berg, Mark Harmon, Adam Arkin. Those actors were like a trio of porn-movie "fluffers." By the time I got off work after a day that entailed love scenes with them, I felt ready to pounce into the sack with my husband.

Years before I met Tommy, when I was filming . . . *And Justice for All*, Al Pacino fluffed for, well, Al Pacino, with whom I went on to have a long affair. Of course, as the quintessential professional, I wouldn't consider dating him until *after* we wrapped the film. The flirtation and chemistry we developed throughout the shoot always had to remain strictly "in character." I felt any potential personal relationship could never interfere with our movie one. But after we wrapped, all bets were off.

Then I worked with one of the greatest fluffers of all time, Bradley Cooper, in *Jack and Bobby*, before he was *Bradley Cooper*. After lying on a dining room table in a slip with a nearly naked Bradley all afternoon, I came home primed and pumped for hot sex with my husband, who was the happy beneficiary.

I know today many young actresses feel empowered by appearing nude. But for me it was the opposite. Back then, I thought refusing nudity was the only way to be regarded as a serious actress. Have I mentioned that respect was a priority for me?

During the filming of *Swing Shift*, my no-nudity rule made a sex scene with Kurt Russell especially challenging. The director wanted to shoot from the angle of my back, so he asked me to take off my bra. I agreed to do it, but only after he swore the camera wasn't seeing any breast whatsoever. However, I got so into the fake love-making with Russell (not hard to do) that I paid no attention to the positions of cameras. When I watched the released movie, my director remained true to his word—not a smidgen of even side boob was visible. But years later, when I saw the "director's cut," which got a lot of play (even though this was way before the days of You-Tube), there they appeared—a full frontal of my breasts, in all their naked glory. I thought at first that maybe the director had used a body double, since I had been so insistent about the no-exposed-breast thing. But then I looked more closely, and sure enough, they belonged to me. I felt betrayed but also secretly relieved that they looked so perky. By that point I was relieved that anything about me still looked perky.

But did that somehow make it okay? If they looked droopy, would I have demanded he remove those shots? Even though it was just a "director's cut," in retrospect, he should have asked for my permission to use the footage. By the time I saw it, though, I'd been nominated for an Oscar for my performance. Maybe I felt I'd garnered enough respect to withstand a little objectification.

I've also done a couple of love scenes directed by . . . my husband. One of them, in *Crazy from the Heart*, depicted my character and her lover in a postcoital embrace on the flatbed of his pick-up truck. Our skin glowed in the light of the fifty votive candles that surrounded us. The romantic Mexican music playing on the radio also helped us get into the mood. Normally a director who does multiple takes, Tommy seemed abruptly satisfied with the very first take this time—"All right, good, we got that . . . let's move on!" Poor Ruben Blades could barely make eye contact with me as he instinctively patted my back and disengaged from our stiff embrace.

But what to do when you have to be madly in love with someone in a scene and you can't stand him? It happens. Sometimes when I have to look adoringly into someone's eyes, I imagine they're the eyes of Nellie, my golden retriever. I'm sure there've been many actors who've looked into mine and thought about their dog or their favorite pasta dish or sports team. There's always something we can find to help us "fall in love."

Unless a person stinks, and then I'm fucked. I have an off-the-charts olfactory sensitivity. So if someone has B.O. or bad breath, I'm screwed because that's all I can think about. Whenever the caterers serve midmorning hot food during shooting, the odor becomes painfully distracting to me. On *Chicago Hope*, if they'd served beans at lunch, I'd have to breathe through my mouth until the crew's fart clouds cleared.

Recently, I had to discreetly ask the assistant of a sloshed movie star whose breath smelled like sad old vodka to please give him some Binaca breath spray right before our kissing scene. Just in case, I put enough in my mouth for both of us. When his eyes watered while we kissed, I wasn't sure if he was moved by the scene or if my mouth spray was setting his eyeballs on fire.

I'm a very dependent kind of actor. I can never act to a piece of tape on the side of the camera, like some cinematographers ask you to do. I have to look at my partners and respond moment to moment to whatever they give me. "Your ouch is only as great as their pinch," my great acting teacher William Esper used to say.

This was a particular challenge for me in one big studio movie. My costar had come to the set so high on something that during my close-ups, he kept dozing off while he sat off-camera. My character, who was secretly falling in love, wanted to make a connection with this man. But as I said my lines, I noticed his eyes rolling up to the top of his head and starting to close. As his head began to bob forward, the cameraman poked him in the shoulder so he would wake up and say his lines. Once I thought I heard him snoring. It threw me so much, I didn't know whether to laugh or cry. Luckily, crying was appropriate for the scene. So I just used the fact that I was having to play a love scene all by myself. That could make a rock weep.

Love scenes can definitely get confusing. Even though you're speaking written lines to a virtual stranger, you can't fake it; you really have to find those feelings. In fact, in my opinion, every emotion has to be real; you can't just pretend to be angry, joyful, sad, or lustful, you've got to really go there. I've often been asked, "How do you *not* fall in love with your costar? Don't fiction and reality ever get confused?"

Sometimes, yes. One time in particular the lines blurred precariously.

On location in Toronto, my coactor and I had several physically intimate scenes together. One of them involved me throwing him down on the bed, jumping on top of him, and ripping off his clothes. This guy was charming, good-looking, and extremely professional. But after we'd wrapped one night, we went out to dinner and the touching didn't stop. We kissed without any cameras rolling. That scared the shit out of me. Not only was that unprofessional, but I had never been unfaithful to my husband in the twenty years of our marriage.

What I adored about this guy was that by all accounts, he appeared to adore me. Or his character did. I didn't know. I didn't care. Either way, he put me high on a pedestal, and the view from up there was fan-fucking-tastic.

The truth is, being on a film set is like swimming in a pool of adoration. You have hair, makeup, and wardrobe people constantly preening over you, ADs who will fetch you anything your heart desires. A bottle of water? Sure! Cold or room temp? With or without a straw? Oatmeal made with water or whole, 2 percent, skim, or almond milk? There are countless crew people who sing your praises after virtually every scene, even if you sucked. Makeup artists will tell you how ravishingly beautiful the lighting is for your close-up, even though they're lying through their teeth. It's heaven on earth, if it's attention you crave.

At that time in my marriage, I was feeling a bit taken for granted. Tommy and I weren't prioritizing each other; both of us were working constantly and not spending much time together. But before we got married, we had made a pact that if either of us ever had an inclination to have an affair, we would first try taking the unfulfilled need back to each other. So I did.

I said a quick good night to my hot-to-trot costar. As soon as I got back home, I knew I had to confess my near affair with my husband. But I felt nervous. Even though he had never been the jealous, possessive type, of course the news would be hurtful. But first I had to figure out what exactly I was missing in my relationship with him.

"So, Tommy, all we did was kiss once, but I was very attracted to him and I'm not sure why. I feel terrible and like I cheated on you, and I'm really, really sorry."

There was a pause. Then he said softly, "Yeah, so am I." He looked away from me.

"Well, what I think I need and am not getting enough of from you is . . . um . . . well, I wish you adored me more, or at least actively appreciated me more."

Tommy said he thought he understood. We didn't speak much the rest of that day or night. He spent a lot of time in front of the TV, watching football. Our normal easy humor evaporated.

Then the next morning he brought me breakfast in bed and rubbed my feet. There was much unsolicited affection throughout the day. He showered me with compliments, and most of them sounded sincere. I think he even washed my car.

All this lavish attention lasted a good solid . . . week. We both ended up feeling silly, like we'd been playing parts in a bad romcom. But fortunately, by that point it had dawned on me that I didn't really need adulation from my husband. I could save that need for award shows, for fawning hosts of talk shows, or for the next time I worked on a film set.

So here's what I wish they'd taught me and my fellow actors in my fantasy love scene class: Sex scenes are going to be uncomfortable, so you need to speak up if there's a boundary issue. Keep it sexy; forcibly doing anything never is. Always carry Binaca, and stay awake. Most importantly, no matter how lucky we are to get to do them sometimes, or how exciting they can be, leave them on the set.

I almost jeopardized my marriage because I confused being adored with being loved. That's like confusing Reddi-wip with homemade whipped cream. Or the "Eiffel Tower" in Las Vegas with the real one in Paris.

It's still nice when once in a while Tommy brings me flowers or kisses my skin as if it's a rose petal. But in the real world, a little of that goes a very long way.

13

Brave

WE WEREN'T EVEN supposed to be in Los Angeles. I'd never wanted to live in that disaster-prone, culturally bereft mini-mall of a city. Whenever I visited, I wanted someone to put a dimmer on the relentless desert sun. I longed to get out and walk somewhere, but there was nowhere to walk to. My husband and I planned to live in LA for just a couple of years to explore film and TV options, but there was no fucking way we were giving up our New Yorker status to be Los Angelenos. Our lack of commitment was made obvious by the various houses we rented with our young children.

Several years later, the offers for the work we came for made it prudent to settle down on the left coast. We bought a home in Santa Monica. At least we would be close to the beach, where we could breathe something other than smog as thick as pea soup.

Once we had officially moved to LA, I began to fantasize about all of the apocalyptic scenarios that could befall us in that dismal part of the country: mudslides, fires, tsunamis, and earthquakes. To soothe my fears, I convinced myself that if a catastrophe were ever to strike me or my family, I'd become a mother lion, suddenly capable of lifting multiple cars to save my kids, and even my husband—who in my fantasy had slept through the whole damn thing. It bears repeating how clueless and comatose my husband is when asleep. I'd have to search our house for any aberrant sounds, armed now with the Maasai walking stick we'd recently brought back from our African safari . . . used to ward off lions.

At the time, my acting roles were for mostly brave, formidable characters: lawyers, doctors, CIA operatives, and kick-ass roles like Annie in *Running on Empty*, Sylvie in *Housekeeping*, and Hazel in *Swing Shift*. Occasionally I got to play more insecure, vulnerable people, but for a while I was being typecast as the fierce female. I mean, people got typecast for a reason, right? I knew better than to identify too closely with my parts, but I started to believe that the strengths of these characters were my own. After playing a doctor for years on *Chicago Hope*, I actually had the impulse to volunteer when a stewardess called for a doctor's assistance on an airplane.

As we settled into our new home, I made sure we had extra flashlights, batteries, and water for possible emergencies. I felt confident I'd rally, just like all my characters would, in any kind of natural disaster.

Six months later, during the magnitude 6.7 Northridge

earthquake of 1994, I got the opportunity to see what I was really made of.

I had been lying soundly asleep alone in our bedroom upstairs when, at 4:30:55 a.m., I was awoken from a dream about being in a massive quake by what felt like a train hitting our house. The shaking of the bed jolted me to the floor. I instinctively found the nearest doorjamb while the room rocked and rolled like ocean waves in a storm. Who knew that floorboards and walls could bend like that?

"NOOOOO! NOOOOOOOO! NOOOOOOOOOOOOOOO!!" I howled at the top of my lungs, as if screaming could stop the tectonic plates from shifting. I wasn't certain at whom or what I was yelling. The noise around me was deafening—glasses and bottles shattering, pictures and mirrors crashing to the floor, the chimney crumbling, car alarms blaring.

Tommy had fallen asleep on the couch downstairs in the den between the twins' room and Wilson's room. I'd never been in a major earthquake before, so I had no evidence that it was ever going to stop. More trains kept slamming into our house. The floor was heaving up and down, lurching and then suddenly dropping. It didn't occur to me to try to make it to the stairs and down to where my children lay sleeping. I only managed to take the one step to our bathroom doorway, whereupon I hung on to the doorframe for dear life. I was frozen, positive not only that my entire family was already flattened downstairs but that I was a goner, too, all in a matter of seconds. So what did I do? I did not, as Dylan Thomas wrote, "go gently into that good night"; I raged and raged and RAGED against the dying of the light!

I can get emotional taking out the garbage, so that should give an idea of the decibel level of my hysteria at the fear that our home was about to collapse on top of us like a house of cards. I couldn't even pretend to be brave. While I screamed like an overly caffeinated banshee, my husband, in a matter of one minute, had grabbed our sound-asleep two-year-olds, Emma and Joe, laid them in their carriers, and put them under the dining room table. When the quaking finally stopped, I tore downstairs, not sure what I would find. I nearly ran into Tommy heading to Wilson's room, whose door had slammed shut during the quake. We threw it open and found our seven-year-old in his Power Rangers PJs, looking scared but unhurt. We held each other and cried as we ran back to our toddlers who had slept through the whole thing.

The aftershocks continued for several hours afterward, during which we squeezed each other's hands and covered our heads. During a moment of calm, I explained to Tommy how grateful I was that he could get to our babies, because given how violently it had been shaking upstairs, there was no way I could have made it downstairs. But in truth, my self-image was the thing most shaken up.

None of this aligned well with the picture I'd cultivated of myself. I learned early on that perfection was the surest path to lovability, a side effect of trying to win my dad's approval my whole life. I saved the only letter he wrote me, sent after the night I took him to the Academy Awards, when I was nominated for Best Supporting Actress. In it, he wrote, "Words can't describe the happiness your mother and I felt." I'm surprised I didn't frame it, nail it to my wall, and surround it with candles.

As a result, it became difficult for me to admit to even the smallest mistakes or to cop to any form of weakness. (I did spend 99 percent of my childhood saying, "I didn't do it!") But the pressure to appear strong and fearless came from me. "No more asking Daddy," as Gloria Steinem said. For so long I felt I needed to be an independent warrior at all costs. Certainly the characters I was portraying would never have behaved like cowards in an earthquake.

I felt secretly ashamed of my behavior for months. I'd learned what "stuff" I was made of and it disappointed me profoundly. I even did research to try to defend my inaction. I found that the upper stories of a house did sway much more forcefully than the ground levels in an earthquake, the same way that the tops of palm trees bend more dramatically than their trunks in a strong wind. I tried to justify my behavior to friends by citing this evidence as we shared our earthquake stories.

"I stayed in bed and lay on top of my wife to protect her," said one.

"I gathered up the kids, the dogs, and the cat and took them all outside," proclaimed another.

"Well, I tried to go down to help, but I was stuck upstairs, which was shaking much more than where Tommy was. See, that's why he could maneuver around so much easier," I said repeatedly. Pathetically.

Finally, I couldn't contain the shame anymore. I didn't know what scared me more, the actual earthquake or being found out for being a chickenshit. So, long after our chimney had been repaired, and all the broken glasses replaced and safely tucked into locked cabinets, I sat down with Tommy at our small kitchen table. Our pictures now hung secured by earthquake-proof putty, yet I found myself still trembling as I broached the subject of my behavior during the quake.

Barely able to make eye contact, I said, "So I lied to you, Tommy. While you were busy protecting our children, I was actually upstairs paralyzed with fear. I probably could have navigated down those steps if I'd tried, but I couldn't move, not because of the shaking but because I was a scared-shitless weenie." I started to cry. "I'm so sorry that I let you and the kids down."

Laughing, he hugged me close and simply said, "Oh, sweetheart, I love you." As he held me, and I revealed my terror, I was taken aback. It was the bravest, most kick-ass I'd felt in a very long time. Maybe I could leave the car lifting to my characters after all.

14

Dear Pregnant Women of a Certain Age . . .

First of all, I hate the phrase "of a certain age." You never hear men say they're "of a certain age." It's absurd. Like women should be too ashamed to ever admit they're over forty? That's like being ashamed to admit you have a cavity or a cold. Should we say "I'm a woman with a certain tooth disorder"? or "I'm a woman with a certain virus"? Aging happens to everyone. If we've survived this long, we should be proud of it.

Anyway, like you, I waited a long time to start a family. Much too selfish and career-obsessed, I couldn't think about anyone or anything else. Perhaps, like me, when you were younger, you weren't even sure you wanted kids. I didn't have my first baby until I was thirty-eight. Then I had a twin set at forty-two.

Well, I feel I should caution you about a few things. I hope you're sitting down. Oh, duh, you're carrying a shitload of extra weight, your ankles have become "kankles," and your acid reflux is so bad it's making your back ache—of course you're sitting down.

By the way, these warnings aren't limited to just you old geezers. All expectant mothers should take heed. But the truths I'm about to share will hit harder if you're older because you are more set in your ways. You've grown more accustomed to doing the things that make your life worth living.

So I don't know about you, but I love to sing and dance. Ever since I was a child, singing and dancing have been my raisons d'être. During my three-year-old tap-dance recitals, my determined tongue always stuck out, pressed against the corner of my mouth for increased focus. At ten I sang along to *South Pacific* in my basement to an audience of neighborhood suckers who paid ten cents a ticket. As the worn, scratched LP played, I burst into *"I'm gonna wash that man right out of my hair!"* with unbridled gusto. As a teenager, after I was supposed to be asleep, I'd put on my 45 rpm single of "Poetry in Motion" or "Run Around Sue" on low volume and practice my jitterbug alone in the dark.

As a cocktail waitress in a large tent in northern Michigan for many summers, I danced while belting out overly sincere versions of "Big Spender" between serving weak Rob Roys and White Russians. When I moved to New York City as a young adult, I adored dancing at Studio 54 and Limelight with my girlfriends and gay boyfriends. I let my body spin around inside the music and get lost in it. We would dance until dawn, leaving the clubs sweaty, dizzy, happy wrecks.

My point is that if you also love to sing and dance, you need to know that once you become a parent, you will never get to do those things again.

You may sing lullabies when they're young. Mine loved "Hush, Little Baby," especially when I'd make up all my own silly verses. My cover of "Baby Mine" from *Dumbo* was also a big hit. I even got away with waltzing around the room with them wrapped in my arms while singing "When I Married Mr. Bill" from *Carousel*. This will exhilarate them, as if you had the pipes of Audra McDonald and the moves of Ginger Rogers.

But they are setting you up. Because the second they get old enough to be embarrassed, you will not, under any circumstances, get to do either without their permission. And I swear to you they will never give it.

"You can sing if I sing," my younger son would sometimes promise, his sweet, rosy face flushed with earnestness. God, you want so desperately to believe him. You pray on a daily basis that he won't renege. But you will find out that he was lying through his retainer-covered teeth. Because even when you've waited patiently for your big moment and dared to sing along *with him* to *his* ridiculous song choice, "Jeremiah Was a Bullfrog," you will hear "Mom! Stop! That's disgusting!"

Until the little control freaks go off to college, you will be in a song-and-dance straitjacket. And by then, if you are like me, it will be too late to start up again; your knees will be arthritic, and inexplicably your voice will have descended into a gravelly baritone, and your vibrato will have slowed down to a pitchy wobble.

You will also realize soon enough that you cannot make any sounds in public, especially within two blocks of their school. I know you're thinking, But I have to be able to talk, don't I? Fine, just speak only when spoken to, and do it very, very softly. But be forewarned that if you ever get too boisterous, you will have to pay big bucks for their therapy later on.

If you're similar to me and have a naturally outgoing personality, you are in deep shit. Because you are who you are by now, and it won't be easy transforming yourself into a soft-spoken, barely breathing mouse. At home, if they have friends over, to be safe, it would be best to just stay in your room with the door closed.

Then there's the whole laughter ruse. I'm aware that my laugh can be over-the-top, often obnoxiously rowdy. But I cherish laughing as much as breathing. Who doesn't? It is one of the most universally therapeutic, spontaneous pleasures of life. When they're little, they will make it seem like you are free to let it rip. The bigger, the better. You can play "mommy-monster," chasing them around the dining table, screaming like a banshee. You get to tickle-torture them endlessly, both of you rolling around the floor, convulsed in hysterics.

But again, this is a cynical con job. Seemingly overnight, this God-given right will be rescinded. You will have to learn to think good and hard before you find anything funny again.

I'm sorry if you think this all sounds like Purgatory. Just wait until you hear this next restriction. Take a deep breath. Okay, ready? There will be *no more skipping*. I know. You're probably thinking, *Skipping?* Who goes out for a skip? I did. It was my gait of choice. I had skipping skills, lifting my knees high, then leaping into the air. It was the closest I could get to flying. Even though as an adult I wasn't supposed to do it, I used to pride myself on the fact that, at least in this one single, solitary arena, I didn't give a shit what others thought of me.

When my children were young, we would skip together, hand in hand, soaring high with great abandon, giggling all the way. But the no-skipping rule became part of the Acceptable Parental Behavior Handbook. After they leave home for college, you can try to skip again. But because by then you'll *really* be an old fart, no matter how hard you try not to, you will pee a little in your pants as you do your first hop. (As a side note, this will also happen while jumping on a trampoline, though not just a little.)

In kids' defense, this low embarrassment threshold is probably a good instinct. They are becoming socially aware. They don't know who they are yet, and we do, so it makes sense they would want us to shut the fuck up and give them some space to figure shit out. It's a healthy kind of narcissism that will eventually be annihilated anyway, as it was for us, once we realized that nobody really cares.

For me this vital life lesson didn't occur until well into my forties. I recall being paralyzed with shame, afraid to go into public places, if I got a negative or even a mixed review on a performance. After I shared this devastating paranoia with my therapist one day, she said, "Hate to break it to you, Christine, but you can count on one hand, and probably even less than that, the people who actually care."

But no matter how painfully long it took you to get over yourself, you will be shocked to find that they haven't. Only last night, I was walking home from a restaurant with my twenty-two-year-old son. Without thinking, for some insane reason, and not without some effort, I started to skip. "What are you *doing*?" he asked derisively, keeping a socially safe distance from me as if I had just urinated on the sidewalk. Which was also true.

Unfortunately, as your kids mature, although you'd expect the reins to loosen up a bit, what you have to look forward to is being ridiculed mercilessly about your behavior *and* your looks. This can get especially agonizing for us more senior moms.

My disses included but were certainly not limited to: my ever-deepening nasal labial folds, the flaccid wattle under my arms, and the peach-pit crepeyness of my stomach that didn't bounce back after my pregnancies. Even though this one was entirely their doing.

Hopefully, as a wiser, more mature parent, you will know not to take any of it personally; your sagging skin must be as thick as a wet suit. But if you are like me, still not quite ready to cuddle up to and embrace *all* your imperfections, you might be kept awake in the middle of the night, full of nagging self-doubt. *Is it rude to send my french fries back, sometimes twice, when they're not crispy enough? Am I overly friendly with fans who recognize me*

*on the street? Am I really tone-deaf? Does my breath smell
worse than vomit? Do I overreact to . . . everything?*

The most disheartening part of all of this was that just
when I finally thought I'd outgrown being an approval
junkie early in my fifties, now I wanted my *children* to be
proud of me! If you find yourself needing that also, well,
don't kill the messenger, but good luck; that's like wanting
your goldfish to be proud of you.

I realize that I've painted a pretty bleak picture here,
and that you may now be rethinking this whole child
thing. Or maybe you're thinking this must all be hyper-
bolic, a perfect example of my tendency to overreact . . .
to everything. I understand. Until you go through it, you
can't possibly know how true all this will be. So let me try
and soften the blow by sharing this recurring dream I had
before having kids.

While walking around my small but adequate apartment, I'd suddenly discover a brand-new door that opened
up into a palatial, magnificent ballroom. I'd lived in this
one-bedroom home my whole life and thought it perfectly
acceptable. But then I came upon this magical space that I
had no idea was there.

I'd never seen a ballroom like this before. Late-afternoon
sun streamed through the massive leaded windows. Towering over polished dark wood floors, the ceilings looked
like they were painted by Michelangelo. It was filled with
beaded crystal chandeliers that made the whole space glow
with an amber light.

Then I had children, and it was exactly like that dream.
And it didn't stop with just that ballroom. With each new

child, I would discover yet another door that would open up to yet another glorious room.

You may not be able to do as much singing and dancing in it, but you simply can't underestimate the value of all that additional real estate. It's the mother lode.

15

Running on Empty

THE CLOSEST I ever felt to my dad was when we sang the Michigan fight song and I helped him pee—not at the same time, mind you. Let me back up and give you some context.

I didn't see my dad much when we were young. He was a general surgeon. "Everything but the head and the heart," he'd explain to anyone who cared. He worked long hours, often called in the middle of the night for emergencies. When he was home, he more or less glued himself to the television, watching sports. Mom would shush us if we ever got too loud. Apparently his games were as high-stakes as his lung cancer operations.

He didn't speak much at family dinners. Isolated at the far end of the long dining room table, he focused instead on cutting and chewing with surgical precision. "Can't talk while the flavor lasts," he would tell Mom and the six of us kids. If one of us ever asked, "Hey Dad, how was work today?" he'd just shake his head, mumble "Hippocratic oath . . . ," and then resume the careful dissection of his roast beef. I'd watch his large, smooth hands work the utensils. Without any wasted movements, they performed their task, and then he'd gracefully place the knife back down before he took each bite.

I had heard how much his patients worshiped him, but to me he was just the boss of our family. I never saw him cry. He never said the words "I'm sorry." Getting praise from him was nearly impossible. One report card with all As and one A-minus was greeted with a deep frown and the question: "What's with the A-minus, Chris—what happened there?" My father seemed more interested in grading his children than in knowing them. Granted, this was a very different era of parenting; being close with your kids wasn't in the job description. Forget helicoptering, our father barely knew our birthdays.

It was hard to find a way in. But when I left for college, I thought I'd found the key. I was Dad's first child to get into his beloved alma mater, U of M. That first semester, we'd meet in Ann Arbor for football games and tailgate picnics of Reuben sandwiches and Budweisers. I got good at pretending to like football.

But only two years later, as a brand-new hippie, I wouldn't be caught dead at a fucking football game. It was right around that time that I was home from college for a visit, and Mom had a lunch with her philanthropic women's group. Dad and I found ourselves alone together, so we decided to take a walk. We went to the parklike grounds of Cranbrook, the nearby private school. It was like taking a stroll with your dentist. We had nothing to talk about. I stared at my feet, wondering what to say, realizing I'd never been alone with him.

"So . . . you think it's going to rain later?" I asked, breaking the silence.

"Yup, the forecast said an eighty percent chance."

"So how's Michigan doing in the basketball playoffs?" I asked, pretending to care.

"Well, they play Ohio State next week, and they have that new shooting guard from . . ."

But I'd stopped listening, because my brain shuts down when it hears sports talk. I wanted to talk about women's rights, about race, about the Vietnam War. I wanted to know if he actually believed, as I had so often heard him state, that "there are no children in America who go to bed hungry." But he'd voted for Barry Goldwater and Richard Nixon, so I already knew his answer. It was like a conversational minefield. No matter what we discussed, it was likely to get explosive. So I said nothing and continued walking silently with my dad, who felt more than ever like a stranger.

After I moved to New York and began to work professionally, there was a real wind shift in our relationship. Right after I was cast in my first movie, . . . *And Justice for All*, before I'd even shot it, he met me at the Detroit airport. A familiar columnist named Shirley Eder from the *Detroit Free Press* happened to be there. Practically accosting her, he said, "Excuse me, but you should meet my daughter, Christine Lahti—she is going to be a very famous actress one day." I was mortified, but I sensed I had found another way in.

As I became more successful, he'd watch everything I did over and over again, he and Mom stuffing massive scrapbooks with every single article ever written about me. Every tiny listing in the *TV Guide* would be treated like it was the front page of the *New York Times*.

When I'd come home for Christmas, he, like the rest of my family, wanted to hear about all the famous people I'd met and fancy places I'd gone to. But from up on an unfamiliar pedestal, this new attention felt hollow, especially coming from my father. He was my number-one fan now, but he felt more out of reach than ever.

I became most acutely aware of this on the way to the Academy Awards when I'd been nominated for Best Supporting Actress. As my mother, father, husband, and I sat in the back of our white stretch limo, Dad fidgeted in his seat and complained about the heat. He had to be proud. After all, I'd finally achieved the biggest prize of all, an *Oscar nomination*, for God's sake. Yet he seemed distant and a bit uncomfortable. As I opened the champagne, he looked over at us and anxiously cleared his throat, saying, "Christine and Tommy. Put your seat belts on, please."

"Dad, we're in the back of a limo. We're fine."

As we all sipped our Dom Perignon, he started to lecture us about the importance of wearing a seat belt. He recounted horror story after horror story of mangled people who were thrown from their cars and ended up in the emergency room or dead because they didn't buckle up.

"If they'd had a seat belt on, they'd have walked away without a scratch," he stated, lighting up his pipe.

"Okay, Dad." I chuckled a bit. "Can we maybe change the subject?"

"You wouldn't be laughing if you saw the guy who came in last week. No seat belt? Ended up in a field somewhere. Paralyzed from the neck down."

Mom looked at us, embarrassed, and kept the champagne flowing. That was our entire conversation for the long forty-five-minute celebratory pre-Oscar ride.

When my mom died at age seventy-five—Dad was seventy-seven—they had been together for more than fifty years. A few weeks after her death, he called me from Arizona. I didn't remember him ever calling me before. He was in a panic.

"Yeah, Christine. Listen, I need your help with something." It was the first time he'd ever asked me for help. I suddenly felt like I was about to fail a pop quiz.

"Uh, sure, what is it, Dad? Are you okay?"

"No, actually, I have a problem. I'm . . . um . . . all out of detergent!"

"Okay, well, why don't you go get some, Dad?"

"I can't. I don't know where to get it."

"Well, Dad, it's going to be okay. You just need to go to a grocery store."

"I can't remember the last time I've been to a damn grocery store. Just tell me! Where the hell do I find the detergent in a grocery store?"

I told him. He thanked me. I hung up. A year later, he

remarried. And that was the end of his reaching out, at least for a while.

A few years into his second marriage, I noticed his hands shaking while he was trying to take a picture of us at the LA County Museum of Art during a visit with his new wife. Then at the age of seventy-nine, he was diagnosed with Parkinson's disease.

During the period before his illness became completely debilitating, Dad joked that one of the positive sides of his memory loss was that he still could watch my *Chicago Hope* episodes multiple times, but now it was as if he'd never seen them before.

Inevitably, Dad's health declined, and just as predictably, his new wife left him. He was now alone, living in a nursing home near my older sister in Florida. Dad also suffered from hallucinations. He had episodes when he imagined that he was once again a medic in World War II and he needed to sew someone's hand back on. Other times he was late for an emergency gallbladder operation. I wondered, when I heard these stories, if he ever hallucinated about us, his family.

When I'd visit him, he mostly just seemed concerned about two things: where his wallet and, even more importantly, where his Viagra was, although he probably had no use for either. In his more lucid moments, he'd ask me, "How do I find a young woman like Anna Nicole Smith? Her old husband was eighty-nine. I'm only eighty-two!" He seemed dead serious.

One warm evening, a few years later, we were at our lakeside cottage in northern Michigan, where we had spent every summer growing up. Dad was now in a wheel-chair. It was sunset, and my husband, brother, and I gingerly lifted Dad's frail six-foot-three body and lowered him into the Jacuzzi on our redwood deck. He moaned as the hot, bubbly water soothed his brittle joints. I watched his surgeon's hands hold on to the edge of the tub. Once so nimble and assured, they were now stiff and quivering, with a life all their own.

There was nothing Dad loved more in the world than sipping his Manhattan while watching sunsets from this deck. When we were kids, he'd call all of us to come out-side, every evening, to make sure we didn't miss one sec-ond. On these humid summer nights, we'd obediently sit with him and watch as the sun sank behind the hills across the lake, its waves finally flattened, as the water mirrored the fiery red clouds. I didn't get to talk to him much, but at least we got to harmonize together. He'd sing, *"Well Irene, goodnight Irene, Irene goodnight."* Then we'd join in, *"Goodnight Irene, goodnight Irene, I'll see you in my dreams."*

Tonight on the deck, though, I looked at his face, cap-tivated by the sunset, and wondered how many more of these moments he'd get to have.

Later that evening, once he was put to bed, his nurse left for the night. I was heading upstairs when I heard the urgent ringing of the little brass bell that sat on my father's bedside table. Dad needed to use the bathroom. I went into his room to help him sit up. I retrieved his bedpan. I gave it to him. About to walk away to give him some privacy, I noticed his hands shaking so hard that he couldn't open up his boxers. He stared at his turbulent fingers as if they belonged to someone else. With great effort, he finally got his penis out of the opening in the shorts, but now his hands were trembling so badly he couldn't aim it properly. His head down, his eyes fixed on the ground, he said, "Take it . . . quickly . . . just hurry . . . put it over the pan . . . now!" I did. He peed. I placed his penis back into his shorts and helped him to lie down, tucking him in.

I turned off the light and walked out of the room. I glanced back at him through the window. His gaunt face looked so naked and frightened as he lay there alone in his rented hospital bed, still so undiscovered. I stood there imagining myself going back in his room, holding him and comforting him to sleep, maybe caressing the paper-thin skin on his forehead. But I couldn't.

The following day, we hardly spoke. I brought him his ice-cold beer as he watched the golf game, the volume turned all the way up.

The last time I saw Dad, he couldn't speak at all. He was only able to make guttural jackhammer sounds, as if words were too painful for him, like spoken pieces of broken glass. He seemed pulled into the horizon of his favorite sunset. I sat with him, trying to talk to him. Nothing. I sang, "*Irene, goodnight Irene . . .* Dad?" No luck.

I decided to make one last attempt. I started singing something we'd sung together hundreds of times before:

"*Hail! to the victors valiant, Hail! to the conquering heroes . . .*" Suddenly, Dad started to sing along with me, clear as a bell, in a full, strong voice.

"HAIL! HAIL! TO MICHIGAN, THE LEADERS AND BEST!

HAIL! TO THE VICTORS VALIANT, HAIL! TO THE CONQUERING HEROES . . ." We finished strong, "HAIL! HAIL! TO MICHIGAN, THE CHAMPIONS OF THE WEST!"

I cheered, shouting "GO BLUE!" I could have sworn he smiled. I wanted more. I held his stiff shoulders. "Go Blue, Dad!" He looked away again, distracted. "No—Go Blue, Dad! Dad?"

But he went back to his sunsets. When I told him that I had to leave to catch my plane an hour later, I stooped to kiss his forehead good-bye. He emerged again without warning. He turned and stared, as if suddenly recognizing me.

"Nooooo," he whispered. I touched his face. We looked at each other for a few seconds. I'd never really noticed how pale blue his eyes were. They grew wet.

"Hey, Dad, don't worry, I'll see you soon. I love you."

AT MY FATHER'S funeral a few weeks later, a stranger came up to me and said, "You don't know me, but your dad was a hero to me. I worshiped him. If it wasn't for him, I wouldn't be here." Then another one approached me and said, "I'm sorry to disturb you, but I have to tell you how incredibly grateful I am to your dad. We all felt so close to him. He saved my mom's life. He was our hero."

I thanked them and walked away. What could I say in response?

Toward the end of the service, I suddenly remembered something that my mother had told me. In the movie *Running on Empty* there's a scene in a restaurant between a daughter, played by me, and her father, who have been estranged for fifteen years because of radical political differences. For me, acting it wasn't exactly an emotional stretch. What I learned from my mother was that Dad had memorized every single line of dialogue from that scene, and often spoke it out loud while watching it. Both parts.

It moved me deeply to think of him bathed in the cold glow of the television, by himself, reciting those lines. He wept. My mom said so. My dad, who never cried, said all the lines and wept.

I'll never understand exactly why my father acted out this scene. I've often wished he could have found a way to express all that loss and regret to me directly. But maybe it was the only way he could mourn what might have been. With his daughter. Whom he barely knew.

16

Panic

XCUSE ME, JOE? I'm so sorry, but I . . . I'm having trouble breathing. My heart is racing," I whispered to my
director. We were on a break during our last rehearsal
before we started shooting the movie *Out of the Ashes*, in
Vilnius, Lithuania. It was 2002, and we were in a large,
brightly lit conference room in our hotel.

"Really? What do you think's going on?" he asked,
alarmed.

"I don't have a clue. I've never felt this before in my
life!" I said, taking in little desperate gasps of air, feeling
as though a large hand was gripping my throat.

"Okay, what can we do? Should we take you to the
emergency room?"

"Yeah, I think maybe I need to see a heart specialist—
like right away!"

A production assistant rushed me to the nearest medical clinic. After examining me and hearing about all my symptoms, the Lithuanian doctor sat me down in her sterile office cubicle. She was a small, masculine-looking woman with short, pomaded hair. She pulled out a heavy blue medical book written in English from her cluttered shelf. She leafed through it, and pointed to a chapter heading that read "Chronic Anxiety Disorder."

I would have laughed if I could have found the breath. Instead I managed to wheeze, "Oh, no, that's not it at all, this is some kind of heart attack or something. Why aren't you giving me an EKG?"

With a slight shake of her head, she tapped her finger on the bold letters at the top of the page. She repeated her command, "Reat dees!"

"Yes, I know, I saw it. But you don't understand—I'm not crazy! There's no way that anxiety could be causing this. I'm a calm person, I never even get stressed out!" I replied, clearly stressed out. She looked at me blankly. Then she glanced at her beloved book again and held it up inches from my nose.

"Doctor, please, this is absurd," I panted, shoving the thing away from my face. "I'm usually incredibly healthy. I work out every day. I have a treadmill in my hotel room. Please just check my heart!" I begged, shivering on my ice-cold prison-style chair.

"Reat dis whole page," she barked in her heavy, dictatorial Lithuanian dialect. "You are hafink a panic attack. Your symptoms are classic. You neet to take Prozac ant Xanax daily ant a strong sleepink pill every night."

Sure enough, every symptom listed on the aforementioned page of her book matched mine.

I was about to film my dream role based on the true story of a Jewish doctor from Hungary who was a prisoner at Auschwitz; while there, she risked her own life by performing countless abortions to save the lives of pregnant Jewish women. I'd been preparing for months, perfecting a Hungarian accent, and we'd just completed a full week of rehearsal in Vilnius. *And now my heart's about to explode through my chest? I can't say a line without losing my breath, and we're supposed to start shooting tomorrow?!*

I left the austere Lithuanian clinic and immediately called my doctor in LA—because, panic attack or not, there was no fuckin' way I was taking all that medication. My LA doctor said that tomorrow I should try just a half a Xanax and nothing else. Then I called my husband, at 4:00 a.m. his time.

"I don't know what's happening to me! I'm going crazy. I can't catch my breath. We're supposed to start shooting tomorrow!"

In a calm, steady voice, he reassured me I was going to be okay and then asked me what he could do.

"You could help me get a ticket home. I need to get out of here tomorrow! Please?" He knew that I had no history of anxiety-related issues and that, as an experienced professional, I'd normally never let anything interfere with my work. "Christine," he said, "you are about to play a Holocaust survivor whose entire family is killed. You're on the other side of the world from your own children. It would be weird if you *weren't* terrified. You can do this,

but you should share what's happening with your director."

He was right. Within the last few months, I'd watched
every single movie and every documentary on the Holocaust in existence. I'd also devoured every book I could get
ahold of. Previously unaware of many of the details, I was
now filled, apparently to the breaking point, with images
of concentration camps, the mountains of skeletons left un-
buried, the emaciated inmates barely able to walk. I was
playing a woman who had to watch the black smoke rising
from the chimney of the crematorium where her children
were being burned to death.

"Really? Tell him I'm having a panic attack because
I'm too inside my character, and as a result I may not be
able to do the scene? I can't. He'll think I'm some kind of
unprofessional wack job!" Unshowered, with greasy hair,
I sat gripping my knees on the cold tile floor of my hotel
room.

I should have known something was wrong when I had
difficulty leaving my room that first week in Vilnius. Usually when traveling I'm a captivated tourist, but I had no
interest in exploring anything. I couldn't even socialize
with the rest of the cast. I just wanted to stay in and watch
more Holocaust documentaries. But that seemed normal
for me when preparing for a challenging role like this one.

If all the extensive research wasn't enough, this was
in 2002, just after 9/11. As my husband reminded me, I
was several continents away from my family. Before text-
ing and e-mailing, the only way of contacting people was
a long-distance phone call, which was nearly impossible

given the extreme time difference. Never comfortable with being needy, I wasn't even aware that I was in trouble. I didn't notice the red flag when I left to get food one afternoon and an unfamiliar dread hit me as I got lost in a football-stadium-sized grocery store. Disorientated, I dropped my bags of apples and pretzels in somebody's grocery cart and left without buying a thing. I was also having violent nightmares and, uncharacteristically, suffering from insomnia. *Jesus, how bad do things have to get before I can admit I need help?* As a psychiatrist later told me after I shared what happened, "You can pretend all you want, but in the end your body doesn't lie."

My husband responded: "No, just tell the director what's going on with you and to please be patient if you need a moment to do your work. You'll feel better knowing that you're not alone with this." I closed my red, swollen eyes and imagined my husband's warm hand holding mine.

I couldn't sleep much that night. The next morning, I took my half Xanax. I got through hair and makeup while going back and forth in my mind, trying to decide what to do. Then, just before we started shooting, I asked the director to come into my trailer and told him everything . . . in a Hungarian accent. We'd made a pact that I would only speak "in character" to him and to the other crew members while on set or in my trailer.

"Joe," I gasped, "dis ees so embarrassink for me to admeet, but I neet to tell you vat iss goink on vit me. . . . Vat de doctorr sait vas det I vas havink an anxiety atteck and det I needed to . . ." Then, after a few minutes of *still* trying to be a good girl, I apologized for breaking the dialect rule—then finished explaining the situation, in my own voice.

"I understand. Don't worry, Christine," he reassured me. "Take as much time as you need. It's even fine if you ever have to leave the set for a while." He closed the door gently. Within minutes, I was finally able to take a much-needed deep breath.

Luckily, once I got through that first day of shooting, I didn't need any more Xanax, although I always kept it with me. By the end of that first week, I could relax enough to try to understand what the hell had happened.

In the five years after that incident, I never had another episode like that one, but I continued to travel with that little plastic Xanax bottle safely tucked into a zipped pocket of my purse, just in case. Once you have a panic attack, you're always panicked that it might happen again.

A critic who reviewed the Holocaust film in *New York* magazine said, "Christine Lahti is the new Glenn Close, a strong woman for all occasions, an adult no matter what." Ha! If he only knew I hadn't a clue what that meant. It had never occurred to me that real strength, the kind that can pull you up off the floor, involves knowing that you've fallen and that you might need a hand. If I had known that, I could have saved a lot of money on Xanax.

And no matter how much I try to delude myself, my body doesn't lie. Even while sleeping sometimes, I dream in character.

17

Brother

WHEN MY OLDER brother died last year, I never cried. As my siblings and I tried sharing some positive memories about him, all I could come up with was that he played a mean game of Ping-Pong. Oh, and that I used to love the stick-figure cartoons he would draw when we were kids.

"Hey, Joe, where's Bob?" asked Sam.

"Oh, he's just hanging around the corner," replied Joe.

The next drawing was a picture of Sam going around the corner only to find Bob, his eyes popped out, hanging by a noose. I laughed until my stomach ached at that joke when I was eight years old.

When we were growing up, our parents lived by the old proverb "Children should be seen but not heard." However, in our house, I'm not sure how much they even saw the six of us. Did they not notice the red flag that my brother waved in their faces when, at only seven years old, he threw that large metal trash can onto the head of our then five-year-old sister?

When I was seven, I dreaded him; the way he'd straddle my tiny body, then drool close to my face. I can still see his spittle snakes slithering closer and closer until they nearly bit my nose. Other times he'd hold me down, put his butt inches above my nose, and fart. He found it hilarious. I just figured that's what older brothers got to do to their younger sisters.

Then when I was around eight or nine, he started beating me up. He hurt our older sister, too. If we heard him coming, sometimes we would hide together behind Mom's garment bags of sequined gowns, afraid to breathe, in that walk-in cedar closet that reeked so much of mothballs that our eyes would water.

Admittedly, I could be bratty. Like that time in the car when I was mad at him and he stuttered. Time always stopped during these frequent stutter spasms. In this instance, it was the "F" sound. His mouth battled with it explosively for several excruciating seconds during which fragments of it shot out like shrapnel—"F . . . f . . . f . . . f . . . f . . . f!"

Sitting in the front seat of our green Buick, I turned around to him. "Stutter butter! Stutter butter!" I taunted. I shouldn't have bullied him. But I'm not sure if that's what even instigated that first beating. Did I tease him because he beat me, or did he beat me because I teased him? Does it really matter?

The specifics of the assaults remain a blur, as if covered

with layers of gauze. But I do remember it would happen at night, when our parents were out. Either he pulled me down the stairs to our basement, or I was already there practicing *Mozart Made Easy* on our upright piano.

I see his red, acned face, the tiny slits of his eyes. There is his large sweaty hand locking both of mine behind my back, while his other one slugs me in the stomach over and over again. There's the burning of his fists through my body, the losing of breath, the cold of the black-speckled floor tiles against my skin.

When our parents finally returned, I'd tell them, but they wouldn't believe me, no matter how forceful or urgent the telling.

"Mom and Dad! Ted hit me!" I'd cry.

"Liar!" he'd say.

"*He's* lying. He almost killed me!"

"I didn't touch her!"

"I swear to God. He pounded me *as hard as he could*!"

Then Mom and Dad would glance at each other. As he turned his back and walked into his office to refill his pipe, Dad would bark, "Both of you go to your rooms and stay there. I don't want to hear another word."

And, as was the custom in our house, that would be the end of words. Gagged, I'd storm up to my room to the solace of my stuffed animals. As my brother followed, I'd hear him snickering under his breath, as though plotting his next attack.

This abuse happened many times, although I can't say exactly how often. I'm still confounded by the fog encasing these memories. How can something so jagged and razor-sharp as trauma become so blunted? But apparently I said "as hard as he could" so often during that period that our parents' only course of action was to ban that phrase from our family's vernacular. When I dared to utter those words, I'd get grounded. Maybe they just thought that if I couldn't say it, then they couldn't hear it, then it didn't happen.

As far as I knew, there were never any repercussions for him. My parents never exactly accused me of lying; they just dismissed it as "normal sibling rivalry" or "boys will be boys." I was also the girl with the too-big feelings, the only emotional creature in our otherwise mostly stoic family. "She must be overdramatizing it," they could have muttered to each other.

But the violence Ted inflicted on me still lives in me. It's become as much a part of who I am as my name. I find that I'm still hypersensitive to people touching me too hard. Even if just in play, if I'm tickled or poked too roughly by my children, that old feeling of helplessness is reignited. His abuse remains visceral.

If I had ever confronted Ted about it, he might have said, "What's the big deal? We were kids. Let it go!" But there have been lasting consequences. Whenever I see a man being emotionally or physically abusive to a woman, I feel the urge to intervene—and I have, sometimes unwisely. His abuse has also fueled my activism, leading me to become a board member of Equality Now, an international organization that fights the global epidemic of sex slavery and violence against women; to speak at marches for women's rights; and to become involved in such organizations as the Equal Rights Amendment Coalition.

If I see men not listening to women or talking over them, my blood begins to boil. Even today, it's still hard for me to trust that I'm really being heard. I find myself sometimes exaggerating things because I subconsciously fear I won't be believed just telling simple truths.

After my husband asked me the other night how many times my brother hit me, I immediately responded "Fifty." Yet it might have happened only a handful of times. I must have still felt, so many years later, that I had to say a number like that to convince him that it happened at all.

The beatings stopped when I was about eleven and my brother was fourteen. Again, I'm not sure why. Maybe because I grew taller than him around that time. Perhaps my newly sprouted body scared him. It's harder to break a tree than a twig.

Ted went after our eleven-year-old little brother a few years later while driving all of us kids to go skiing. When our younger brother hit him back, Ted pulled the station wagon off the road so he could pummel him outside in the snow. We four girls couldn't watch. Grateful it wasn't us, we just sat in the car, focusing even more intently on keeping our legs stick-straight so the new stretch pants we'd gotten for Christmas wouldn't bag in the knees.

For a couple of years in high school, Ted and I grew a bit closer, although only superficially. Mostly, we just used each other. When my parents went away for weekends, he'd organize huge keg parties in our basement, hire a band, and, always the entrepreneur, charge $4 for admission. He invited me because I knew some of the "popular" people he desperately wanted to be friends with. At sixteen, I thought it cool to be able to drink beer, dance, and flirt with older guys. One Sunday morning my parents came home unexpectedly early and discovered a couple of Ted's sloshed guests passed out in the sauna. This time there were consequences for both of us.

Things really started to unravel for my brother after he started pre-med classes in college. Because he was Ted Lahti *Jr.*, my dad expected that he'd follow in his footsteps and become a doctor. But Ted never wanted that. What he really strived for was Dad's approval. For him, that became an unachievable lifelong obsession.

I shared that goal with him, but the bar was not as high for me. Since I was a girl, my status equaled that of a non-VIP—but in my family, the pressure for Ted to succeed, as the firstborn son, must have been viselike.

After having a nervous breakdown, Ted dropped out of med school. With Dad's financial help, he proceeded to get into real estate, and within a few years he made millions of dollars. At long last, Dad seemed proud of him. Once, during this period, Ted came to a party I had, opened his wallet, and flashed his wad of hundred-dollar bills to all of my unimpressed, bewildered hippie friends.

Just two years later, after making many ill-advised real estate deals, Ted lost everything, including the $100,000 that Dad had invested—much of my parents' retirement money. Needless to say, that loss put an irrevocable strain on their relationship. Ted threatened to sue our father; he even pulled one of Dad's guns on him while Mom, cowering, in the corner, pleaded for him to put it down.

Out of desperation, Ted started writing bad checks, got caught, and called me collect one day to tell me that unless they were paid off, he'd have to go to prison for two years. He was broke. No way would Dad bail him out again, so he had to turn to me—his only sibling, at the time, who could afford it. I gave him the money, but in retrospect, who knows how much of that story was even true?

Then, in his mid-thirties, he went through debilitating depressions and heavily self-medicated with alcohol and drugs. While drunk driving one night, he rolled his truck in a Michigan cornfield. It landed on top of him and cut him open. His organs fell out of his bloated belly. He spent a week in the ICU. He survived but left the hospital with a scar that slung across his torso like an angry purple banner.

Soon after that, I came face-to-face with his delusions and mania for the first time. There was that visit to New York City, when he swore he had an appointment with Walter Cronkite. He didn't. He'd recklessly take walks in Central Park at 4:00 a.m.

Then he showed me his drawings: meticulously detailed plans of sound stages he proposed we build in Hawaii for my fledgling career. He said I needed to put up the initial investment, but that he'd already lined up several other interested parties, and we could make whatever movies we wanted in our Hawaiian mini-studio. Sitting together on the imitation Persian rug in my tiny studio apartment, I stared into his furtive eyes, trying to ascertain whether he'd become a pathological liar or had truly begun to lose his grip on reality.

We all begged him to see a psychiatrist. He'd insist that nothing was wrong. Finally, after years of pleading, he agreed, but reported back that the doctor had diagnosed him as "only" having "borderline personality disorder." None of us knew what that meant. I remember feeling relieved. Well, at least he's only *borderline*! He'd found his defense. "See? Like I've been telling you! Nothing to worry about!" He insisted that it was meaningless and that no therapy, treatment, or medication had ever been recommended. His well-honed gift of denial kept him from seeking professional help.

He adamantly refused to find employment, except for the occasional house-painting gig. "I'm not the type who can work for someone else," he would say. Instead, he supported himself through the "barter system," by mooching off others, and by manipulating people.

At this point, I didn't fear him anymore. Instead, I just felt responsible for him. Not only was I the sole person who could "lend" him money, I felt the need to protect my parents from him. I hated the pain he'd caused them, especially my mother. She had her hands full enough trying to cope with my younger sister, who'd developed severe bipolar disease during this period. I can still picture Mom sitting alone, in the dark, in the refuge of her immaculate, all-white living room, while her world outside crashed and burned.

For years we implored Ted to stop harassing them, to quit lying, to go to rehab, to admit he needed help and see a therapist. Time and again these confrontations, fueled by my naive arrogance that I somehow had the power to change him, proved futile. Many nights I'd be unable to sleep, my throat raw from having spent hours trying to reason with a drunk, as if my anguished pleading could ever have penetrated his tequila-sodden skin.

He never ended up getting a job, but he spent decades working on archetypes for a solar train and an eco-village— brilliant, innovative ideas that mostly stayed trapped inside his overflowing notebooks. For years, before computers, he'd send me letters: long, single-spaced handwritten missives blaming others for everything that had gone so wrong in his life. Drawn with multicolored Sharpies, his intricate drawings and frantic plans could never escape from their pages.

Except for the checks I'd send him, our communication devolved into only his steady stream of e-mails, which detailed his current conspiracy theories and the latest, definitive dates of the end of the world. He warned us over and over again that we should buy gold coins, purchase guns, get out of urban areas, and find underground shelters. I finally begged him to stop. I'd had my fill of the apocalypse.

During this same period he sent me a home video that crushed me. He'd filmed an "interview" with Mom and Dad during a visit to our family cottage. In it, Ted asked them if they were happy he'd come home, why specifically they were glad he was there, and whether they loved him. He repeated the questions over and over again. He was around fifty years old at the time.

I didn't hear from him for quite a while after that. But whenever I saw an emaciated homeless man on the street in Santa Monica, I'd have to look away, fearing it might be him. They all looked so much like him. They still do.

The last time I saw him, I had invited him to stay with us for Thanksgiving out of a sense of familial obligation. He arrived with his thinning hair greasy from not having showered, wearing smelly clothes, with holes in his shoes. Instead of a suitcase, he carried a wrinkled trash bag. He'd told us he'd been diagnosed with thyroid cancer and that it had spread into his back. We couldn't tell if that, too, was yet another lie. Barely saying a word, he spent the entire three days laying on the couch, drinking Coors, reading trashy magazines, and watching soap operas.

He'd periodically write to me, calling me his "angel," his "only friend." But by that point I wasn't his angel or his friend. "Chrissy, thanks for being the only one who cares. Love, Teddy." I knew he just needed more money. At nearly seventy years old, always knowing there'd be someone to bail him out, he remained a child. Even at the very end, I felt obliged to support him, to keep him from having to live in his car as the very real cancer ate away what was left of his bones.

In one of his last letters, he wrote, "I don't know how my life ended this way. I feel like I was a good person." I know he had goodness. But mostly I remember him as a person crippled by mental illness who couldn't be rescued.

He died alone, in a rented one-bedroom condo with a busted coffee table and a stained mattress. His only possession was Dad's old beat-up Mercury, filled with cans of tuna and green beans, cases of water and a gun. A survivalist who couldn't survive. A scam artist who got away with nothing. A con man who, in the end, tried but failed, to con his sister out of caring.

18

Monster

Excuse me, but there's a really creepy guy wandering around, and I think he's stalking me. Would you mind if I just hung out with you guys for a minute?" asked a visibly frightened young woman, approaching my husband and me as we unlocked our storeroom.

"Of course. Stay here with us," we whispered back as we peered up and down the labyrinth of spotless corridors, trying to see who the hell she was talking about.

I'd never been in one of these huge storage facilities before. It looked like a mausoleum, with endless hallways lined with thousands of padlocked garage doors. The only light came from long tubes of fluorescents that buzzed on as you entered a particular aisle.

We didn't see anybody. I thought for a split second that maybe this woman was just paranoid. Then suddenly we heard it: the scraping of shoes on cement, the kind you imagine in your worst dark-alley nightmares, from the next hall over, getting closer and closer. The beast emerged, then galumphed past us, staring straight ahead, stone-faced.

He looked like Frankenstein, a very low-budget horror-movie version. His features seemed stuck on with paste, the kind I used to eat in first grade. Unevenly placed, his ears hung uncertainly from his massive head, upon which teetered a too-small Dodgers cap. One of his eyes was looking at you. The other was looking for you. The expression on his face told of the recent terror of having just chopped up his parents, put their body parts in plastic trash bags, and stuffed them into the family freezer in the basement.

Well over six feet tall and leading with the backs of his hands, he lumbered away slowly, like a zombie in a Saturday-morning cartoon. His arms grazed his knees, and his feet dragged as though trying to escape from the rest of his body.

"Ahhh. Okay, yeah, I get it," I said quietly. "If you want, I can stay with you while you get your stuff out." Instinctively, I wanted to protect her. This woman couldn't even accomplish a simple task like getting camping gear out of her storeroom because of this menace. I started thinking about all the streets I'd avoided, the elevators I'd let go by, the words I hadn't been able to speak, because of my own man-fear. When we first entered this place, I'd told Tommy it should be called a House of Hoarders, but now it seemed more like a House of Horrors.

Grateful, she led me to her room, only a couple of rows

away from ours. I stood guard while she unlocked her door and found her sleeping bags. I felt strong, even a bit heroic. Of course, I owed my bravura entirely to Tommy's close proximity.

I knew better than to think my presence alone would in any way discourage this man. I thought of college, when my girlfriends and I brazenly hitchhiked through Europe, utterly impervious to any danger. Three women strong, we assumed no one would dare mess with us. However, the middle-aged, pudgy German who picked us up proceeded to grab our thighs and grope under our skirts while driving too fast on the Autobahn. Finally, after whacking his insistent, entitled hand away from our bodies and screaming, "Stop, auto!" over and over again, we convinced the audacious motherfucker to pull over, and we all escaped. That night we slept in a field, only to wake up to an irate farmer bounding toward us through the tall grass, yelling and wielding a shotgun.

The nervous woman and I made small talk about her planned trip to Joshua Tree while she pulled out her tent and foam pads. Then, without warning, the creature rounded the corner and plodded toward us again. Heart instantly galloping, I dropped my calm facade faster than you can say "coward" and called out to my husband, my voice rising a few octaves higher than Minnie Mouse's, "Ahh, Tommy! Would you come here for a second, please?" I instinctively looked down, avoiding any eye contact, like I'd read you're supposed to do when encountering a bear. Tommy hurried over just as the man shuffled by us once more.

"Jesus, talk about right out of central casting!" I said

under my breath, trying to laugh it off. But that familiar dread crawled up my spine, gripping the back of my neck. Still, I decided I would accompany my new friend to the elevator while Tommy stayed alone with our stuff.

As we followed the exit signs through the tangle of tunnels, she thanked me. "I'm not usually such a scaredy-cat," she said. "But a few months ago, at a 7-Eleven, a guy walked by me on my way in. I didn't pay any attention to him. But as I headed back to my car, he came up behind me and slugged me in the back of my head, sending my glasses flying. He screamed, 'Now you know who I am, bitch!'"

I touched her shoulder and held it for a few quiet seconds. Her fear fueled mine. After she had safely entered the elevator, I traveled back alone through the empty passageways to find our room. At every intersection my body stiffened with the prospect of this creep popping out right in front of me.

"Tommy! Where are you?" I called again. He answered, and I followed the refuge of his voice. While walking to him, I remembered an incident in New York City when I was being stalked. It was late at night in a residential area. I sensed someone following me. I turned around and saw an older dark-haired man walking very close. I crossed over to the other side. He crossed too and came up right behind me. I did the only thing I could think to do: I started to act stricken with some horrible deformity. I dragged my foot. I shot my hands out spastically, murmuring to myself, "GRNFMMMMMAWAAAHH." This stopped him. He turned around and headed the other direction.

My breath quickened as I traveled down another long hallway. Was I going to have to pull out my pretend-I'm-insane defense again?

When I finally found Tommy, he informed me that while I was escorting the woman, he'd gone up to the guy and asked him if he needed help. The man had taken a step closer toward him, bugged out his crossed eyes, then walked away without a word.

How the hell did Tommy have the courage to do that? To approach the man would not have occurred to me. *Talk* to him? Are you fucking kidding? And risk him (1) lunging at me, (2) raping me, (3) killing me, or (4) all of the above? I began to well up.

While Tommy lifted our heavy boxes, he tried to reassure me. The man had to be just a mentally challenged adult, possibly homeless and disoriented. I found myself jealous of Tommy's comfort level. He didn't understand that my tears flowed not only from immediate fear but also from the acute realization that women just don't get to feel safe.

My husband didn't have to live in such a constant state of hypervigilance—on subways, walking through parks, in bars, at work, in empty storage buildings. He'd never experienced even the more benign harassments that women are forced to endure on a daily basis—the lewd remarks, the unwanted touches. They all add up to a lifetime of little razor cuts. Tommy had never even been scratched.

Few men I know have tales of assault. But us women are constantly wary; being female in a sexist culture means lower status on the food chain. I learned early to be on guard because of an abusive older brother and a predatory, sexist casting director. No wonder a fiendish-looking man lurking in a storage asylum freaks me the fuck out.

My tears fell for my twenty-three-year-old daughter. She has to deal with some kind of aggression almost every time she goes outside. I had so hoped the world would be ready to welcome her power. But the looks and comments she gets from men on the street are hurled at her like weapons.

I cried for my friend in college, who was raped at knifepoint. I found her, in shock, lying in bed, right after the man fled her unlocked, trusting home in Ann Arbor, Michigan.

I relived the beatings I'd endured growing up, at the fists of my older brother. I've never gotten over that powerlessness. Most women don't. The violence inflicted on us lives in us; absorbed through our skin, then etched into our bones. Every time a strange man gets too close, it resurfaces and we flinch, detour, hide, walk faster, run, duck and cover.

Standing near my husband, I maintained a vigilant eye out for the creep, certain that peril lurked merely a few feet away. Then suddenly we heard him whimper from the next hallway over, like the cries of a confused, wounded animal, more hopeless and heart-shredding than any I'd ever heard. My husband and I looked at each other. Holy shit. Maybe he was just an innocent, mentally challenged person who somehow wandered into this metal maze and didn't know how to get out.

My tears came back. This time for him. At the sound

of his whimper, the prospect of his unmitigated loneliness gutted me. Every time he walked down a street, I imagined people scattering away from him, like from a pressure cooker found in a dumpster. Really, this helpless man-child, simply born into a permanent Halloween costume, needed my empathy, not my fear.

The moaning stopped. We heard his footsteps scuff toward the elevator. We closed our door, locked it, loaded up our cart, and took the lift upstairs. As we exited the building, we found him again. One of the storage facility workers, who had a huge, goofy smile on his face, held his hand as he escorted him into the restroom. Jesus. Had he just been looking for a toilet this whole time?

Perhaps in the future if I see someone who needs help, I will stop, take a breath, and try to figure out if my fear is justified or simply the bleeding of old wounds. I'd like to think that if I ever go back to Culver City Storage and see that man again, I might ask him his name, or even help him find his way. Maybe next time I won't be such a monster.

19

Mamma Mia

M Y DAUGHTER AND I are singing, as we skip, arm in arm, down the aisle, *"Mamma mia, here I go again. My, my, how can I resist you?"* We're about to see this Broadway musical together on a warm Sunday afternoon in New York City. She's seven years old and recently played the lead role in her after-school children's theater production, where she was so *perfectly* cast as Donna, the forty-something, divorced single mother of a twenty-year-old.

We've planned this trip for months, filling the dates on our kitchen wall calendar with stick-on silver and gold stars. Now, just minutes from entering the enchanted, promising world of the Greek islands, I'm about to turn off my phone when, out of the blue, my younger brother Jim calls me from Dallas. He informs me that our sister Linda ingested a huge amount of lithium last night.

"They're pumping her stomach right now, but they said

if all goes well, she should be okay," he says over the din of hospital bells and the urgent paging of a doctor.

"But what happened, Jim? I mean, why would she take so much lithium?" I whisper, my level of denial breaking all previously set records.

"Ah, well, I think . . . you know, I think . . . she tried to kill herself."

"LADIES AND GENTLEMEN, WELCOME TO MAMMA MIA!" The audience erupts.

"Oh shit, I've got to go Jim, I'll call you back at intermission."

"PLEASE SILENCE YOUR PHONES, AND WHY NOT UNWRAP THAT HARD CANDY NOW?"

The applause gets louder. The overture begins playing.

Jesus Christ, this can't be happening. I look down at my daughter; she's spellbound. Of course I'm not going to tell her anything. I can't. Not now. She looks up at me, and I flash her a smile, then try to focus on the stage. I can't see anything but blinding lights. The music builds to a deafening crescendo. Wait, stop, don't they understand?! My baby sister just tried to . . .

"*You can dance, you can jive . . . having the time of your life!*" sing the actors onstage, having the time of their lives.

Holy shit. One of the *Lahtis* attempted suicide? This isn't supposed to happen to any of us. The Lahtis never give up. No matter how formidable the obstacle, we persevere! We wear "Lahti" like a badge of honor—my surgeon dad, my beautiful stay-at-home mom, six perfect children. I mean, it's clearly displayed on our annual Christmas cards, all eight of us professionally photographed in our

all-white living room, placed like perfectly arranged flowers, everyone in their red outfits, all of us beaming our
orthodontically enhanced smiles—those smiles that safe-
guard all our secrets. *Merry Christmas! We are the Lahtis,*
gosh darn it, and we are an enviable, happy motherfucking
family!

But now my mentally ill sister is in a hospital, strug-
gling to stay alive. When we were kids, if any one acted
"crazy" it was me, not Linda. Though the youngest, she
seemed the most mature. She'd often go down our long
hallway at bedtime, checking in on the five of us. *I* was the
child who had the hysterical mood swings, the crying jags,
hiding under our dining room table while the rest of my
stoic family sat and ate their dinner. Between my wails, I
could hear them snickering, making fun of me—everyone
except Linda.

One time I ran upstairs, slamming the door so hard my
palomino china horse fell from its shelf. I heard a knock
on my door.

"GO AWAY AND DON'T EVER COME BACK."

"It's Linda, Chris."

I let her in. My sister gently picked up shattered bits of
horse tail and then sat on my bed, softly rubbing my hand.
"It's okay, Chrissy, it's going to be okay."

I wish I was sitting on her bed right now, rubbing her
hand saying, "It's okay, Linda, *you're* going to be okay,"
instead of sitting here in the Winter Garden Theater.

"See that girl, watch that scene, digging the dancing
queen . . ."

I look down at my daughter, who looks radiant, sitting

up straighter than I've ever seen. I try to remember my sister when she was around Emma's age. I can't come up with much. Maybe because I was too busy trying to make her my "pal."

"Pal" in my family was a euphemism for slave, in a game invented by us three older siblings to ensure that the three younger ones would help do our chores. But more importantly to me, since I hated being alone, it guaranteed I'd have a playmate. My other sisters (Carol and Cathy), brothers (Jim and Ted), and I all clamored for Linda as top pal/slave, because she would likely be the most obedient. There would always be a fierce bidding war for her.

"Hey, Leelee, come here for a sec," I'd beckon from the corner of the upstairs hall that connected all of our bedrooms, holding out my half-eaten pack of Lik-M-Aid as if it were a bag of gems. "If you'll be my pal for this week, I'll give you the rest of this and half of my Pez," I whispered.

"Well, hmmm, actually Ted already offered me all of his—"

"Okay, fine! All of my Pez *and* my wax lips. But here's the deal—you have to play Barbie and Ken dolls with me, help me clean my room, and go to the corner store with me to get more Lik-M-Aid since you're taking—"

"Well, I'm not really taking your Lik—"

"Don't interrupt! That's not very nice pal-like behavior!"

"Okey-dokey, we're pals!"

Yes! She was mine! I felt like I'd won a trip to Disneyland. I didn't think to ask her what she felt about it. None of us did. She was the youngest, the quiet, sweet runt of a loud, demanding litter.

Then once the rest of us had left for college or to start our adult lives, she was the only kid living at home for a couple of years. She was a senior in high school when she called me. "It's really weird, Chris. It's so quiet and empty here in this big house. I feel like everyone's left me. I mean, who's going to be *my* pal?" I'd not heard her express many needs of her own before. So that next summer, we hopped in my orange VW Bug and I took her on a road trip to visit our older sister, Carol, in Colorado. Linda was in high spirits the entire twenty-hour drive.

"How many miles have we driven, Chris? Because we could split the driving, you know. Let's see, if there are a thousand miles left to Colorado and you've already driven three hundred, then we could split the remaining seven hundred—that would mean, let's see, three hundred fifty miles a piece, oh wait, but since you've already—"

"Leelee, whoa, have you had a lot of coffee?" I asked, laughing.

"No, I'm just so excited to be taking this road trip with you, and I want to make sure we split the driving time equally so—"

"Hey, listen, Carole King's playing, your favorite!" I interrupted. She loved to sing, and I knew that *Tapestry* was her favorite album. "*'But you're so far away'*—harmonize with me! *'Doesn't anybody stay in one place anymore . . .'* Leelee, sing!"

But she just went on and on about our mileage sharing. I thought, Well, maybe she's just making up for all those many years when she happily let the five of us do all the talking.

Once we arrived in Colorado, I asked my older sister, "Hey, Carol, do you notice anything different about Linda?"

"No, not really. She just seems really *up*, you know, really perky."

"Yeah, you're right. She's fine."

Our gift for denial was clearly a family contagion.

Six months after our road trip, during Linda's second semester as a freshman at U of M, I received a frantic call from my mom. "Christine, Linda's had some kind of psychotic breakdown. She thinks she's been impregnated by God! They found her on the steps of the student union, and they called me to pick her up." She went on to explain that when she arrived at the school, the university security guards coaxed Linda into the back seat of Mom's car. On the way home, our shy sister took off all her clothes, and for forty-five minutes she screamed at the top of her lungs, "GODDAMNSHITMOTHERFUCKINCOCKSUCKINPIECEOFMOTHERFUCKINFUCK!"

Linda refused to go to a hospital, so Mom was forced to call the police.

"Oh, hello, Officer, yes, my name is Betty Lahti. Oh . . . fine, thank you, and yourself? Good, well, I'm so sorry to bother you, but I have a little situation over here. My daughter seems to be—"

"Shitfuckingfuck!" Linda spit out her words, her sweaty hair glued to her face.

"Shhh, honey!" whispered Mom. "I'm sorry, Officer, I'm actually in a bit of a bind here, my daughter's having some kind of . . . honey, please put your clothes back on!"

Linda started moaning, swaying back and forth like a rocking chair.

"I'm so sorry, Officer, but . . . could you get over here, please, AS SOON AS POSSIBLE?"

The police arrived. Helpless, Mom watched as they forced her daughter into a straitjacket and hauled her, kicking and screaming, to the local hospital psych ward. That day, as my little sister broke down, so did the myth that we Lahtis somehow floated above the fray in our pretend suburban bubble. This was our breaking point. No amount of smiling could make this one go away.

"YES I'VE BEEN BROKEN-HEARTED, BLUE SINCE THE DAY WE PARTED . . ."

I look over at my daughter; she's singing softly under her breath. She looks back at me. We've sung this song together a hundred times. I take her small hand and sing along.

". . . MAMMA MIA, WHY, WHY DID I EVER LET YOU GO . . ."

I put my arm around her and breathe her in. I forget the words. How did my family live under one roof for so long but hardly ever see each other? How many other signs did we miss? I rarely noticed Linda having a mood, let alone a mood swing.

"She's schizophrenic, no, she's psychotic, no, she's bipolar!" The doctors didn't know what the hell she was, so they gave her Thorazine—buckets of it, apparently, because when I saw her many months later I hardly recognized her. Having just come home from the hospital, Linda came into my room. Her twenty-year-old face was so puffy from the medication that her skin looked stretched and shiny like a balloon. Her blond hair was brown from not having been washed. She'd gained seventy pounds and was shaking and shuffling.

"Well, Chris, I guess, it turns out that . . ." She suddenly lost her train of thought.

"That what, honey?"

"Oh, that I'm, uh, bipolar. They think it's from the hash that I smoked the night before my first breakdown, but the doctor said that it was, uh . . ." She drifted away again.

"Linda? What did the doctor say?" I asked, trying to bring her back.

"Oh yeah, that it was possible that I may have developed this anyway, even without the hash, but he said . . ."

"Wait, they think the hash triggered it?"

"Yeah, apparently hash and grass can do that. They don't know for sure, but he said . . ."

"What, sweetie?"

"Oh, that if I take my medication, I should be able to get stable and, you know, be okay."

Oh my God, I thought. Would she be okay, or was she going to spend the rest of her life in a mental institution? Would I get this? This was hereditary, right? I had extreme mood swings. I'd not only smoked weed, I'd taken LSD and psilocybin mushrooms. How the fuck could I still be okay while my sister was severely mentally ill? Jesus, please let her be all right, I prayed. She had to be—once they figure out the right medication for her, she'd be okay. A lot of people were bipolar, and they were able to have successful, rich lives. She'd have the best doctors, Dad would make sure of that. And Mom would make sure she always took her meds and stayed balanced.

The next year there were no more manic incidents, but Linda seemed muted, more subdued and slowed down, almost as if submerged in sludge at times. We'd talk a lot on the phone, and I'd see her for holidays. She didn't complain much, but it was clear that she had to put great effort into pretending to enjoy the festivities. Then I got a call from her.

"Chris, I'm going to California. I want to try to find Carole King!" she announced with the old enthusiasm and energy she'd lost since her breakdown at college.

"Honey, come on. You're going to look for Carole King?"

"No, not really. I want to see friends out there. But wouldn't it be great if I ran into her?" She laughed.

We thought maybe her doctors had finally found the right medications for her. What we didn't know was that she'd stopped taking them.

She told me later that with the help of a "Map of the Stars," she actually found Carole King's house and knocked on the door. When no one answered, she decided to wait in the rented car all day, until finally Ms. King drove into the driveway and headed inside with several bags of groceries.

Linda leaped out and introduced herself. Then she

paused for dramatic effect. Startled, Carole turned and stared at her.

"You know, *Linda Lahti*," my sister repeated. "I'm the girl you've been writing about all these years!"

"Huh? Excuse me?" asked Carole, shielding her eyes from the California sun.

"'When you're down and troubled and need a helping hand?' . . . How did you know? *Tapestry* . . . that whole album is about me. 'So Far Away'? Well, I'm not anymore, I'm here!"

"Okay, what was your name? Linda?" shouted Carole, keeping her distance. "Look, this is private property, all right? And you are trespassing, so you need to get into your car right now and—"

"No! No, you don't get it, I came all this way just to thank you for understanding me and for writing all your songs about—"

SLAM. Carole escaped into her house. Linda got out of there just before the police arrived.

"Waterloo, couldn't escape if I wanted to . . ."

Now people are getting up, dancing in the aisles. I attempt to dance, too, but it seems I have someone else's arms and legs attached to my body. I sit back down. All I want to do is call my brother. I glance at my program. Ah, it's the last song before intermission. I sneak a look at my phone for messages, but there's nothing.

Finally. Blackout! The curtain comes down. The house lights come up. I turn to my daughter, whose face is lit up like a birthday cake.

"Oh, Emmie, I know, this is so amazing, right?"

"Mommy, are you okay? Don't you like it?" whispers my daughter. Nothing escapes her.

"No, sweetie, I love it." I feel the sting of my lie. "I just . . . well, I got an upsetting call about Aunt Linda before the show. Actually, I want to call Uncle Jim really quickly to make sure she's okay, so would you mind going to get us some M&Ms? Here's some money. It's right up there, and come right back, okay?"

The phone is cold in my hands. "Hey, Jim. What's the news?" I ask, waving at my daughter up the aisle.

"Well, they're saying it looks good—I mean, they can't be sure, but they're hopeful. They said she's resting now, and if everything goes well, the family can talk to her in the morning."

"Oh, thank God!"

My daughter returns from her candy mission. "Thank you, honey!" I say, hugging her. She wraps her body around me like a small blanket.

"How's Aunt Linda?"

"She's doing better! They said she's, uh . . . oh, it's starting!" The house lights go down. The music comes up and . . . Mamma mia, here we go again! My arms glued to the sides of my body in a chair that was designed for tiny people, I try to think back to the first time my sister might have felt she'd be better off dead than alive.

"I have no thoughts, Chris, I can barely get out of bed taking all this stuff. They've tried everything, nothing's worked. I'd rather be manic than be brain-dead," she confessed to me after the Carole King episode, during the next of her many debilitating depressions. But I didn't see that as a red flag, just another huge bump in the road. I knew her to be, like the rest of our family, a fighter; tenacious and unsinkable.

Linda once said that after a while Dad didn't really want to listen to her complaints anymore; about trying to lose weight, finding motivation . . . to do anything.

"Where there's a will, there's a way," he would lecture her. "Just work hard, hold your head up, smile, and be friendly."

He never believed she needed therapy for her bipolar disorder. "Not necessary. Just stay on your medications and you'll be fine."

Mom would accuse him of being too tough on Linda, reminding him that she was mentally ill, not lazy. When he refused to send Linda extra money, Mom would mail her secret checks.

"You're doing more harm than good by coddling her," he'd say. "She'll never be independent if you keep treating her like a baby."

But ever since that first episode on the steps of the student union, she'd always managed to be a warrior of resiliency. No matter how many times she'd been knocked down and flattened by her illness, no matter how many emotional roller coasters she'd been forced to endure, she'd always declare, "Chris, I'm going to do it this time. I'm going to finally lose these hundred pounds no matter what. I'm going to stay on my meds from now on. I have to just accept that this is a part of me and remember, as Dad taught us, to always just—you know—'buck up!'"

Then there would be many long periods when she did

seem fine, or relatively fine. One time after she'd moved away from Michigan to Dallas, she got her own apartment, held down a job as a receptionist in a large office, and completely supported herself. She called me from work.

"Chris, guess what? You're not going to believe this! I finally have some good news! I just won the Worker of the Month contest at my job, and they're putting my picture on the front page of the weekly newsletter!"

She said it with the pride of a Nobel Peace Prize winner. She also joined a weekly group therapy session, where she met Erick, a young man with multiple-personality disorder who would become her best friend and roommate. I think she liked being the caregiver for someone else for a change. She adored him, looked after him, and found him endlessly entertaining. I never knew which Erick would answer the phone.

"Hello, this is Erick, who am I speaking to p-p-p-p-please?" he'd ask shyly, in a high-pitched voice.

"Hi, Erick, this is Christine, Linda's sister."

Then he'd switch to flamboyant, enthusiastic super fan. "OMG, is it really? Oh, Miss Christine! I LOVE YOU! Ahhhhh! I can't believe I'm talking to a real live Hollywood movie star! Could you send me your autograph, please?"

Or sometimes I'd call and get the monosyllabic, withholding tough guy.

"What?"

"Hi, Erick, this is Linda's sister. Is she there?"

"I don't know."

"Well, uh, do you think you could look?"

"Whaddya want?"

"Well, I'd like to—"

"I don't know where she is."

"Well, could you give her a message that I—"

Click.

Linda would say, "Hey, I'm lucky! I get five roommates for the price of one!"

Even when she was depressed, she would pretend otherwise. "I don't want to bring everyone else down," she used to say. But her eyes always betrayed her. They remained muddy and lifeless, no matter what role she tried to play. At times she seemed to drift off into some private dark lake, alone and out of reach.

But somehow, in spite of everything, she managed to have a sense of humor about herself. When questioned about her California stalking adventure, she'd respond, "Oh yeah, Carole King and I go way back!" I would be reminded of something photographer Diane Arbus once said: "Most people go through life dreading they'll have a traumatic experience. Freaks were born with theirs. They've already passed their test in life. They're aristocrats."

But no matter how long Linda's periods of "stability" lasted, I'd eventually get a call.

"Christine, can you call Al Pacino for me? Like today? It's really important. I have an idea on how to remake . . . *And Justice for All*." She sounded out of breath, like she'd been sprinting.

"Uh . . . sure, Linda, but you know it's still playing in the theaters, right?"

"No, I know, but I think the ending is all wrong. Al shouldn't be in the courtroom like that telling—"

"Honey, are you taking your lithium?" I interrupted.

"Yes! Oh, and I need to talk to the Supreme Court justices—do you have their phone numbers?"

"Yeah, let me just get my Rolodex!" I said, trying to humor her. "Honey, what are you doing right now?"

"Ah, well, actually, I'm putting all the rubber bands on my counter here in a line, and ordering them by color, size, and elasticity."

"Sweetie . . ."

"Uh, sorry, Chris, I've got to go, David Letterman is trying to reach me." This particular manic episode became so severe it landed her in the psych ward again.

This time they couldn't bring her down from her mania, no matter what amount or combination of medications. So Linda called and informed me, "They've run out of choices, Chris. They want to try electroshock therapy." Horrified, I instantly pictured Jack Nicholson's character in *One Flew over the Cuckoo's Nest*, but she assured me that EST had come a long way since that movie, that it was now state-of-the-art and extremely effective. She ended up having it done several times—once to get her down from that mania, twice to bring her up from depression. Although she'd lose her short-term memory temporarily, it always seemed to help, but not for very long.

Then, just a few years ago, on her fortieth birthday, she finally made a real commitment to never go off her meds again. "If I do, I'll have to go through this whole cycle again and I can't. I can't deal with another one, there's just too much wear and tear on my soul . . . ya know? I don't have a choice really," she declared.

But it didn't matter. The mania actually broke through the lithium. My brother found her walking in the middle of rush-hour traffic, trying to get a check to Bill Clinton to "help him save the world."

Then, after this episode and nine months of yet another severe depression, Linda told me that, inexplicably, her doctor had let her know that if this new "cocktail" of drugs didn't stabilize her, he'd be out of options. There would be nothing else for him to try.

We spoke just a few weeks before she tried to end her life. I'd phoned her from LA.

"Hey, Lynn, how're you feeling?"

"Well, actually not so good . . . These latest meds aren't working. I've lost my thoughts again, I can't even get out of bed, and my doctor said—"

"I know what that asshole said, honey. We'll find a different doctor. They're going to figure this out, sweetheart, don't worry. You're going to be okay, you always are," I said, repeating the same old tired refrain.

"Yeah, I know, but also . . . Erick moved out last week. He had to go back home to be with his family."

"Oh, shit, Lynn, I'm sorry."

"Yeah, me too. It's a little lonely here without him. I mean, I know it'll be fine, but I guess . . . well, to be honest, I'm pretty down about it. And not that I would ever act on them or anything, but the last few days, like for the first time ever, I've been having some suicidal thoughts." She said it like she had been thinking of getting her car washed.

But the word hung, unmoving, in the air. "Suicidal"

was taboo; never, in the twenty-five years of her illness, had that word escaped past her Lahti smile. The avoidance of it felt instinctual, like the need to look away when passing a crushed dog on the side of the road.

"Wait, what are you saying, Linda? Seriously?"

"No! Don't worry, Chris, they're just thoughts, not like a plan or anything . . . nothing more!" she insisted, extinguishing the words as quickly as she'd ignited them.

"Okay, but are you sure you would never, in a million years—"

"No, never. I promise. That's not an option for me, that will never happen!"

"Linda, you're going to get through this, okay? You have to trust that!" I said, sounding a lot like our parents. "You know I'm here for you always, right?"

"I know. Don't worry. I'll be okay," she reassured me. I suddenly pictured her, our perfect little sister, going from room to room down that long hallway to make sure we were all okay.

There was a pause. It could have been for five seconds or for thirty-five. Then one of us changed the subject. I don't remember who. Of course I don't. It's much too painful to imagine that it could very well have been me.

I believed her. I had to. The alternative was unthinkable. I trusted that she would find her footing again, like she always had. I actually thought her confession helped her somehow . . . you know, like those little earthquakes that let off just enough pressure to prevent the big one?

"*Schoolbag in hand, she leaves home in the early morning*," the actress sang softly from the stage.

Sometime after we spoke, things must have gotten so bad that she decided she'd had enough. I tried to imagine that day. When she woke up, maybe she didn't see the sunlight that flooded through her drawn floral curtains. As usual, she had to lug herself out of bed. She didn't think to play a Mozart string quartet or a Joni Mitchell song; even they'd long since failed to stir anything inside her. She could barely look at her Carole King poster, as if it was a former friend who'd betrayed her long ago.

She took a shower, but as usual the hot water didn't soothe her. She washed her hair but didn't bother to rinse enough to get all the soap out. Instinctively she started to blow-dry it, and then the absurdity almost made her smile. She began to put on the deep-red lipstick she'd splurged on months ago but instead dropped it, opened, into the dirty sink. She even tried to force the diamond ring that Mom had given her onto her bloated finger, but the effort exhausted her.

She fed her cat extra food and then hugged her tightly but didn't notice the warmth of her body or the tenderness in her purr. She thought for a second about having her usual plain, nonfat yogurt but instead ate what was left of her four-cheese pizza from the night before. She couldn't taste it, so she threw it away. Anyway, it didn't matter, it was important that she had an empty stomach. Nothing mattered anymore except her plan.

For a moment, she considered calling Erick or Jim but knew there would be no comfort in their voices, no hope left in their claims of love. That had dried up long ago. She ran through the short list of people she used to value, but none of them could distract her from her mission. Besides, she hadn't been able to really picture anyone for quite a while. Her despair was pure and blinding. It had even turned her turquoise walls, painted to match her beloved lake in Michigan, into a dull gray.

Perhaps she opened a few windows to air out the smell of garbage she'd neglected to take out. Maybe she stepped over the pools of clutter on her floor to unlock her door so she could be found more easily. But what were her final thoughts before she got that tall glass of water and opened the three large bottles of lithium that she'd been saving up? Was there one last flicker of promise when a car drove by, blaring music that used to make her weep? Did she urgently try to recall just one person or thing that used to make her laugh? Did she wonder in those final moments if she mattered to anyone?

Or maybe she was unaware of anything but the urgency of her clear, singular purpose: to end the pain, finally just end the pain. So she swallowed all of the pills, carefully wrote down her bank account numbers, instructions that my brother could have her car, and that whoever found her, to please notify her therapist and take care of her cat. Then she got into her bed, pulled her comforter over her, and just . . . waited.

"SLIPPING THROUGH MY FINGERS ALL THE TIME, DO I REALLY SEE WHAT'S IN HER MIND . . ."

But the doctors said they were hopeful; that if all went well, we could talk to her in the morning. But what will I say to her? I'm going to fly to Dallas tomorrow, but what if she doesn't want to see me? What if she's devastated to learn that her suicide failed? What do I say to her then? *I'm so sorry you tried to kill yourself, but we've decided that you can't. I hope you don't mind, but you're going to have to continue with this life that you've already determined to be unlivable.*

How am I going to try to convince her that being alive is worth it? Isn't this something she gets to decide?

Then, as the show ends and the curtain calls begin, my brother phones me. I pick up. "She didn't make it, Chris," he tells me. "Her heart just stopped."

I can't hear the orchestra. I can't hear the applause. I can only see in my mind a photograph of my sister. She is at her kindergarten graduation, her long blond hair blowing beneath her tiny white tasseled cap. She's laughing. With her eyes squinting into the sun, she's looking slightly off to the side, as if distracted by the limitless possibilities of her life.

The audience has leaped to its feet to give a standing ovation. Surrounded by screams of "Bravo, bravo!" I can't help but think, Brava, my little sister. Brava, you tried so hard—for so long.

With Emma pressed close to my side, my arm cocooned around her, I walk slowly up the crowded aisle, softly singing to myself:

"THE FEELING THAT I'M LOSING HER FOREVER, AND WITHOUT REALLY ENTERING HER WORLD, SLIPPING THROUGH MY FINGERS ALL THE TIME, SLIPPING THROUGH MY FINGERS ALL THE TIME."

Then I take my daughter's hand and hold it as tightly as I can.

A FEW DAYS later, all of us siblings gather in Dallas for her memorial. Our parents have already both passed. Of course our sister waited for them to go first. Jim and I go to clean out the small wood-framed house that Dad bought for Linda. It's like a hoarder's home. Each room is filled with stacks of old magazines, notebooks brimming with plans and strategies, and hundreds of travel brochures. Cockroaches crawl over everything. On her nightstand I notice a wrinkled note next to the book *The Power of Positive Thinking*. I open it slowly, holding my breath. Inside are her last words.

I couldn't beat the illness this time. I've lost my soul and my thinking. My mind just won't go on. I wish I didn't have to end my life but this illness has taken its toll on me. I'm so sorry. Please forgive me.

Maybe her last day was the opposite of everything I imagined. Perhaps she woke up that morning feeling more strength and clarity than she had in years because, at long last, she, not her mental illness, had control. I think of the countless days, weeks, possibly years, she might have spent trying to come up with reasons *not* to kill herself.

I carefully fold the note back up and put it in my pocket. Across the room in a corner, I see a collection of miniature lighthouses. I never even knew she collected those. How perfect, I think . . . lighthouses, with their beacons of safety for those who have lost their way. Most of them are dark, although there are a few that flicker on and off. But in the back, behind all the others, I notice one very simple, elegant, white-shingled lighthouse covered with tiny dead cockroaches. It shines with a faint but steady light, its batteries refusing to die.

20

Waiting

AM A MIDDLE-AGED actress. In Hollywood, that's like saying you're mold: toxic and invisible. Hollywood's glass ceiling of ageism is virtually unshatterable. So how did I, this kick-ass, feminist activist who wouldn't take shit from anyone, deal with that? I did the only logical, proactive thing I could think of: I grabbed my phone and called . . . a plastic surgeon. And another. And another. And another— because so far, I've never been able to follow through with it.

In the reception area, waiting to meet with a brand-new doctor for my tenth consultation, I hide behind a *People* magazine. My head starts to spin. I look at my watch: it's already been an hour. *Okay, as long I can get out of here in thirty minutes, I'll be able to jump on the 405 and still get to the rally in time.* I glance around the room. Jesus, don't they have a private waiting area for celebrities? I slide farther down into my chair. *Just don't make eye contact with anyone*. But no one is looking at me anyway; they are all buried in their magazine articles about Jennifer Love Hewitt's exposed cellulite. I want to make myself a nice Roma Nespresso at the coffee buffet, but I don't dare get up. I'm trapped in a waiting-room prison.

A new inmate walks in. Shit, it's an actress I worked with last year. I don't want her to see me here. I drop my magazine onto the coffee table, inadvertently looking down into the table's mirrored surface. I nearly shriek. Oh my God, when did I become a Shar-Pei?

I hightail it into the bathroom and lock the door. With the overhead fluorescent lighting, I know better than to even glance in this sadistic mirror. I close the faux-mahogany lid on the toilet. I sit down and hold my melting face in my sweaty hands. *What're you doing? Why do you keep making these idiotic appointments? This is against everything you believe in! Remember your proudest moment, when Rush Limbaugh called you a feminazi? What the hell are you doing hiding in the bathroom of a Beverly Hills plastic surgeon's office?*

Somebody knocks. "Sorry—be right out!" I flush the toilet, just to sound busy. I bend over, fluff my hair extensions, slip on my Oliver Peoples sunglasses, and slink back into the waiting room. I check in with the receptionist again.

"So sorry, Ms. Lahti, but the doctor's had a few emergencies this morning, so he's running a bit behind," she says in a nasal, upper-crust British accent.

Why does every fucking receptionist in a plastic surgeon's office sound like Maggie Smith? This woman is probably from Brooklyn. And what emergencies? Did a nose fall off? Did a boob pop? I flop back down in my upholstered chair in the corner, burying my head in an *US Weekly* magazine. Flipping through, I count a hundred pictures of stars with nose jobs and fake breasts in designer gowns. I think back to my very first consult, for a nose job the summer after I graduated from high school.

My dad had arranged the appointment back in Detroit with a plastic surgeon friend of his. The previous summer, a local modeling agent had announced that she'd only represent me if I got a nose job. It had never occurred to me that there was anything wrong with my nose. This doctor didn't quite get it, either. So I left deciding that I'd just live with mine, despite its modeling-career-killing deformities. I may have asked the surgeon, however, if there was anything he could do to make me shorter. He laughed. But I think I meant it.

Then after a long, blissful consultation break, at forty-three I went in for one about a boob job. I had just finished breastfeeding my twins, and my breasts looked like a couple of deflated balloons. I had two options—I could just make peace with them, or I could get some "restorative surgery." Certainly there was no harm in putting them back as they were? I could've still been a card-carrying feminist and have done that, right?

But still ashamed about my plan, I told no one. I quietly did my research and talked to three different doctors (all men). They each did the "pencil test."

"When a pencil is placed under a properly suspended breast, it should fall to the floor. However, if the pencil remains under the breast, surgery is highly recommended," they advised me.

I failed the test miserably every time. They brought out a variety pack of implants. I wanted the smallest, most natural ones that would still do the job. I wanted to be the one woman on the planet with completely undetectable implants. I scheduled the surgery.

Then, the day before, a girlfriend who'd had hers done came over to my house to ease my anxiety. She lifted her T-shirt.

"Look, Christine, see how real they look? Go ahead and touch them."

Really? I thought. She wants me to touch them? I was forty-three, and I know I went to college in the 1960s, but I'd never touched another woman's breast before, that I remember. Okay, I thought. This is weird, but kind of cool, I guess.

She laughed. "Don't be afraid, they won't bite." They were perched so high on her chest that she could have used them for a chin rest. "See how soft and natural they feel?"

I patted something that felt like an overly inflated basketball.

"Uh, uh. Wow. Yeah, you're right, totally." I dug my hands back into the safety of my pockets.

That evening I had a nightmare about having to wear an extra-large puffy coat to hide my Dolly Parton–size fake boobs while speaking at an event for Barbara Boxer. As I spoke, my chest got bigger and bigger until I started to rise above the podium. As I floated above a sea of horrified, judgmental women, I began to scream. I woke up drenched in sweat. But it's my body, I told myself. I can do what I want with it!

The next morning, however, still terrorized by the Dolly Parton dream and that friend's basketball boob, I canceled my surgery. Several months later, my breasts actually went back to almost normal all on their own. So, doctors, you can take your No. 2 pencils and shove them where the sun don't shine!

But I look back and wonder . . . what was I so scared of? I had no plans to ever display my breasts onstage or screen, or to anyone but my husband, for that matter. Could I not feel sexy anymore unless I had Barbie-doll boobs? Was I going to let gravity determine my self-esteem? As I grew older, I really didn't give a shit that my breasts had drooped a little. In fact, at least in the boob department, I felt sexier inside my authentic, albeit aging body.

However, I'm now in the waiting room for my tenth consultation about my turkey neck and dangly face. I pick up *US Weekly*. *Great, Jessica Simpson lost eighty pounds in three days. Wait, how did she . . . ? Jesus.* I drop the magazine on the floor. The waiting room is now full. It's time to throw my weight around. Don't they know who I am? I walk up to the receptionist again. "Excuse me, how much longer? I'm in a huge—"

"I'm so sorry, Ms. Lahti, but the doctor's running a—"

"I know, you told me. 'A bit behind,'" I mumble to myself. Goddamn it! I walk over and make myself a coffee. I see some candy in a crystal bowl. As I eat my fifth mini Tootsie Roll, I break out in a sweat and have a sugar-induced flashback.

———

I'VE JUST SAT down with a group of women at a big round table. It's a Beverly Hills fundraiser luncheon for Hillary Clinton, who is running for senator. We are in the dark, listening to a boring speech given by some very cut-up rich older lady. I'm two white wines in when I lean over to my table and blurt out, "You know, as we age, I figure we have two options: we can either look old or we can look weird like that, right?" I tip my glass toward the speaker as I sip my drink, clueless. "Well, I'm going for looking old. When I see someone so obviously nipped and tucked, it seems like she's just wearing her fear on her face, don't you think?"

Crickets.

The woman sitting next to me, her face unmoving, says, "Well, honey, I'd rather look weird." Then the eight other stretched, puffer-fish faces turn to stare at me, nodding, trying their best to smile.

BACK IN THE waiting room, suddenly, the door opens. A beautiful young woman walks in. She looks at most thirty-five. The woman sitting next to me catches me watching this young woman.

"I know, youth is wasted on the young," she whispers. "I'm Catherine. It's okay. I recognize you. I'm an actress too. What are you here for?"

"Oh, nothing, no. I'm not really here. I mean, I'm here, but not for anything. Just like a consultation or something. I have a . . . a questionable mole on my back," I say as I pick up a *People* magazine.

"Yeah, sure, right, me too. But let's admit it, women our age, it's about time we do a little something-something, am I right?" She chuckles.

I'm about to laugh with her when an older woman with a swollen, catlike, severely pulled face enters. "Oh my God. I know her," I whisper to my new actress friend. "She was a famous sitcom actress about twenty years ago. Wow, talk about a cautionary tale." Catherine looks over. She is about to gasp when I go on, "But you know, it's not her fault. She didn't do that to herself. Our fucking culture did it to her!"

"I get it," said Catherine. "I've been having a fight with my face for years."

"Me too, but won't it just get worse if no one ever sees a real, mature female face on the screen?"

"You know what? You're right. We should all go on a plastic surgery strike! Fuck the patriarchy!"

A harried nurse sticks her head into the room. "Catherine?"

"Ah, gotta go! Time for my nip!" She gathers her coat and purse. "Good luck with that . . . mole."

Every muscle in my back is seizing up. I go back to the receptionist. Before I can say another word, she sings, "You're next, Ms. Lahti."

"Shh. Thanks!" I duck back into my little corner. I try to stretch a little. Do I really want to do this? What about all the actresses who've had too much work done, and that's what ultimately, ironically, has ruined their careers? It's so fucking unfair I want to cry, but I can't; it would ruin my three layers of Dior Black Out mascara.

But what's so wrong with just a subtle little lift? I've been fine with the Botox and fillers I've tried. Well, mostly fine. No matter how little I used, I never told anyone except my husband, who thought I was crazy. Then there was that lovely time I became allergic to a filler that the doctor swore was nonallergenic. Instead of looking younger, my skin looked like the surface of the moon.

But come on, Christine, you've dyed your hair for a hundred years. You've pierced your ears. Your lashes were put on by a Korean lady on Fourteenth Street! Why is this such a big deal?

In spite of the fact that all these doctors told me I'd just look "well rested," like I went on a vacation, I've never seen a facelift that doesn't look like, well . . . a facelift. When I see those people on-screen, I'm not looking at their faces, I'm looking at all their "work." So if I just want to keep working as an actress, is it better to look old but real or to look younger but strange? One doctor told me recently that I looked "haggard." Another said it was definely time for surgery because "the covers had fallen off the bed." Ugh, enough! Why does any of this fucking matter?

I look at my watch for the fiftieth time. I have to go. *Fuck it. I'm done with these stupid consultations. I am not mutilating myself for the sake of some oppressive idea of beauty!* I know I've said this before, but I mean it this time. I am going to try to age gracefully and be at peace with my sagging face as I carry it around Hollywood in a wheelbarrow.

I rush up to the desk. "Look, I can't wait anymore. I'm going to be so late for this—"

"I'm so sorry, Ms. Lahti. Would you like to reschedule?"

"Yes . . . no . . . no, I don't . . . I don't actually want another appointment." And with that, I run out of there as fast as my sixty-three-year-old SoulCycled legs can carry me.

I get on the 405 and drive like a lunatic. I park illegally. I dash backstage. It's a get-out-the-vote rally focused on women.

"Oh, great, you're here! You're on!" says a young woman wearing a headset. I rush up the steps of the stage and stand before a giant audience of mostly women.

"Ahhh, hi! Thank you all for coming!" I say, out of breath. "Sorry, I'm late. I was stuck in the waiting room at a . . . a . . . never mind. Anyway, I'm here to help, um . . . empower women! One of the best ways we can do that is by voting next week! Did you know that in every election there are millions of women who don't vote? Your vote counts!" The audience starts to clap, and I catch their energy. "Your voices matter! We can't wait anymore for men to value us. We need to value ourselves AS WE ARE! What are we waiting for?"

The crowd applauds. I look down. Shit, there's a line of press in the first row. I didn't know there were going to be TV cameras here, and shooting from below? I stand there, my hand resting casually under my chin, wishing I didn't care but secretly missing my little invisible adhesive neck "lifts."

I quickly finish my speech. Just as I am about to escape

the tyranny of the cameras, a song starts blasting through the huge speakers.

WHAT YOU WANT, BABY, I GOT IT. WHAT YOU NEED,
YOU KNOW I GOT IT. ALL I'M ASKING IS FOR A LITTLE
RESPECT, JUST A LITTLE BIT . . .

I scan the audience. All the women are singing along and dancing. R-E-S-P-E-C-T, FIND OUT WHAT IT MEANS TO ME!

After about a minute, I step off the stage and drift into the middle of the electrified crowd. R-E-S-P-E-C-T . . .

. . . and with my arms reaching to the sky, I start singing and spinning around and around, my hair in a tempest around my flushed face, as hopeful and . . . undecided as ever.

I GOT TO HAVE . . . JUST A LITTLE BIT . . . A LITTLE
RESPECT . . . JUST A LITTLE BIT . . .

R-E-S-P-E-C-T

ACKNOWLEDGMENTS

HAVE MANY PEOPLE to thank for encouraging me to take this journey and for supporting me along the way.

First and foremost, my husband and life partner of almost thirty-five years, Tommy Schlamme, who not only encouraged me every day but read almost every draft of every one of these stories and gave me invaluable feedback. My daughter, Emma, who was the first to suggest I might have some worthwhile stories to share and to start writing them. My sons, Wilson and Joe, who also greatly inspired me. Jessie Nelson, Kathy Najimy, and Gloria Steinem for their brilliance and for leaving me breathless in the wake of their belief in me as a writer. Calvert Morgan for his early, much appreciated support. Michael Moore, Bryan Gordon, Lisa Kron, Mark Poirier, Di Glazer, Alan Zweibel, Philip Himberg, Robin Morgan, Brian Mann, and Rob and Michelle Reiner for their insightful feedback and encouragement. My amazing writing coaches, Elena Karina Byrne, and Xeni Fragakis. My book agents, Laura Nolan and David Kuhn, and Sarah Levitt for their wisdom and editing talents. My kick-ass, remarkable editors at Harper Wave, Karen Rinaldi, Sarah Murphy, and Hannah Robinson. Robin Hirsch at the Cornelia Street Café Downstairs, Shanta Thake at Joe's Pub, Maggie Rowe and Jill Soloway at Sit N'Spin, Paul Crewes and Justin Masterson at The Wallis Annenberg's Sorting Room, Eva Bernstein at Beyond Baroque, and Terry Mintz from "Word" for letting me develop and workshop many of these stories at their fabulous venues. Danny Goldstein, John Cerna, Carolyn Cantor for all their support and guidance during these readings. Finally, I want to thank my parents for teaching me that if you work hard enough, the sky is indeed the limit.

ABOUT THE AUTHOR

CHRISTINE LAHTI is an acclaimed director and stage, television, and film actress with a career that spans over forty years. She won an Oscar for her short film, *Lieberman in Love*, an Oscar nomination for *Swingshift*, a Golden Globe Award for *No Place Like Home*, an Emmy Award and a Golden Globe Award for *Chicago Hope*, and an Obie Award for *Little Murders*. On Broadway, she starred in *God of Carnage* and *The Heidi Chronicles*, among many others. Some of her films include *Running on Empty* and *Housekeeping*. TV shows include *Jack and Bobby*, *Law and Order SVU*, and *The Blacklist*. She lives in New York City and Los Angeles.